ALSO BY JEREMY BERNSTEIN

Mountain Passages
In the Himalayas

ASCENT

*The Invention
of Mountain Climbing
and Its Practice*

REVISED EDITION

by Jeremy Bernstein

A TOUCHSTONE BOOK

Published by Simon & Schuster Inc.
New York   London   Toronto   Sydney   Tokyo

Touchstone
Simon & Schuster Building
Rockefeller Center
1230 Avenue of the Americas
New York, New York   10020

First Touchstone Edition, 1989
Published by arrangement with University of Nebraska Press
TOUCHSTONE and colophon are registered trademarks
of Simon & Schuster Inc.
Designed by Irving Perkins Associates
Manufactured in the United States of America

10   9   8   7   6   5   4   3   2   1 Pbk.

Library of Congress Cataloging in Publication data

Bernstein, Jeremy, 1929–
    Ascent : the invention of mountain climbing and its practice / by
Jeremy Bernstein. — Rev. ed., 1st Touchstone ed.
        p.   cm.
    Includes bibliographical references.
    1. Mountaineering.   I. Title.
GV200.B498   1989
796.5'22—dc20   89-37572
                                                                    CIP
ISBN 0-671-68275-X Pbk.

Except for the Introduction, the contents of this book appeared originally
in *The New Yorker*.
Excerpts from the following are reprinted with permission:
The Swiss and Their Mountains by Sir Arthur Lunn. Copyright 1963 by
George Allen and Unwin Ltd. Published in the United States by Rand
McNally and Company.
Vocation Alpine by Armand Charlet. Editions Victor Attinger.
Les Aiguilles de Chamonix by Henri Isselin. B. Arthaud.
Edward Whymper by F. T. Smythe. Hodder and Stoughton, Ltd., London,
1940. By permission of Christy and Moore, Ltd.

Contents

Preface

The first three chapters of this book were written in the early 1960's, just after I had discovered the French Alps. They have about them, I think, the romantic enthusiasm of early love. I have decided not to change that tone, but to let the rest of the book act as a commentary. The only thing I have done to these chapters is to fix a few facts. On the other hand, in rereading them, I was struck by how many of the people mentioned have died in the last twenty-five years. I decided not to break into the narrative by pointing that out as I went along. But I would like to use the opportunity of this preface to memorialize Nicolau Barthélémy, Armand Charlet, André Contamine, Gaston Rébuffat, Lionel Terray and, above all, my wonderful friend John Noxon. Noxon is the unnamed physicist/colleague with whom I climbed Memorial Hall at Harvard that moonless spring night in 1955. He and I shared digs in Cambridge whenever he was not off climbing somewhere. We kept in close contact and I miss him greatly. Claude Jaccoux, who figures largely in these narratives, is, as of this writing, organizing a climb of Mount Everest and still guides, climbs, and travels with undiminished élan. As for myself, I haven't given in to the temptations of middle-aged indolence yet. As these words are published, I expect to be in Rwanda with Jaccoux climbing and trekking in the Mountains of the Moon, fulfilling another childhood travel dream. As Kipling wrote in "In the Neolithic Age":

> Still the world is wondrous large
> Seven seas from marge to marge . . .

—Jeremy Bernstein,
New York, April 1989

Introduction

As man's dominion over nature has become more nearly complete, his aesthetic standards have changed. The Northern Lights and lightning are objects of beauty if one understands them, and objects of terror if one does not. For at least a century and a half, it has been taken for granted that mountains—especially snow-covered mountains—are beautiful, and it comes as something of a surprise to learn that throughout most of the history of the human race, mountains have been despised, loathed, and dreaded, and their inhabitants regarded as cursed and doomed. Today, when the Alps are crisscrossed by ski lifts (there was even a rumor that a *téléphérique*, a mechanical lift, to the top of the Mont Blanc, the highest mountain in Europe, was being planned) and when people travel thousands of miles just to look at the great snow walls of the Himalayas, it is almost impossible to understand how snow-covered mountains could ever have been anything but objects of beauty. In this book, and in *The New Yorker* articles on which it is based, I have tried to describe how and when this change in attitude came about.

Most of the book is set in the Chamonix Valley, in the Haute Savoie in France—one of the most magnificent mountain settings I have ever seen. It is the place where mountain climbing was born. It is also in danger of being ruined. There is now a tunnel under Mont Blanc, which adjoins the valley, and there is a superhighway leading from the tunnel in the direction of Geneva. Most of the people in the valley earn their living, in one way or another, from tourists, and the prospect of even more tourists pouring through is, for many, a pleasing one. In the summer of 1964, I met a man who typified, for me, the evolution of the valley. He told me that he and his family were in the shipping business but that they had decided to build a new *téléphérique* in Chamonix as a speculation. Their *téléphérique* had been in operation for a few months now, he said, and it had all but transformed the area it served; what had been a tedious glacier walk for mountaineers was now a ski run. However, it had not been a financial success. The better-known *téléphériques* skimmed off the tourists—the biggest class of customers—leaving him mainly with skiers and climbers. Even so, the long-range prospects looked good, since, as he reasoned, there will soon be so many people in the valley that many of them will not find room on the other *téléphériques*, and people who want to go up something—anything—will have to resort to him. He was a nice man, and it was hard not to wish him well.

Along with the change in aesthetics has come a change in

the practice and popularity of mountaineering. To most Americans, mountaineering is, at best, an extremely eccentric sport. Among Europeans, on the other hand, climbing is quite a popular sport. Books on the subject are often bestsellers, and the more famous Chamonix guides earn a substantial living by writing and lecturing. It is especially popular with intellectuals. Why this should be, one can only guess. Among French physicists, for example, a surprisingly large percentage are climbers. Georges Bonnevay, one of them, was both an excellent physicist and a climber. He was killed in a fall in the summer of 1963 while climbing the north face of the Aiguille de Bionnassay, a beautiful ice peak near Mont Blanc.

I first met Georges in the summer of 1960. We were members of the small faculty teaching physics at a summer school on the island of Corsica. Since we were the only bachelors on the faculty, in the course of things we found ourselves thrown together a good deal. Georges was a frail, somewhat eccentric-looking fellow in his middle thirties, with a long, almost Oriental beard. An excellent artist, he had hesitated a good deal between physics and art before choosing physics. He was the last person I would have imagined to be a climber. In fact, when he told me that he was going to the Chamonix Valley to climb when our summer school was over, I could hardly believe him. I had passed through the valley as a tourist, and the mountains had looked so formidable to me that I considered them beyond the powers of anyone except professional guides and acrobats. Georges told me that not only did he climb but almost all the physicists I knew—teachers and students— had tried climbing at one time or other. Georges was a wonderful raconteur, and his adventures came brilliantly alive when he described them. Perhaps I am wrong, but I think the sheer folly of climbing appealed enormously to his

15

sense of humor. The idea of being on a vertical ice face in the dead of night, delicately picking his way by flashlight along a thin trail of steps chopped in the ice, was to him—at least in retrospect—a gesture resplendent with defiance and whimsy.

When Georges left Corsica, he urged me to come to Chamonix, too, and promised to introduce me to his friends among the guides. I could not get to Chamonix that summer, but during the winter we exchanged letters. He got married that winter, to one of the secretaries at our summer school, and the next year he and his wife had a son. Mutual friends told me that Georges had all but given up climbing after his marriage. Then, in 1963, I ran into a group of French physicists buying equipment in a sports shop in Chamonix, and they told me that Georges, who had been teaching in Paris, was planning to spend his summer vacation near Chamonix with his family and would soon be climbing again. I looked forward to seeing him, but before we could meet he was killed. His death made a deep impression on me. Apart from anything else, it convinced me once again of the extreme dangers involved in climbing, even for climbers as skilled and experienced as Georges was. I decided that I myself would never climb anything really difficult without a guide.

This book grew out of my experiences with the Chamonix guides. They are, by any standards, a remarkable group of men, and I am deeply indebted to them not only for teaching me something about mountaineering but for their kindness in helping me with the material for the book. I am especially indebted to Nicolau Barthélémy, the Chief of the Guide Service, who put up with my endless questions with the greatest kindness and good humor. I am also indebted to J. P. Bernazet and his wife, and to Armand Charlet, André Contamine, Henri Dufour, and Roger Frison-Roche, among many other guides, for their help. Above all, I am indebted to Claude Jaccoux and his wife. Claude, one of the crack climbers in Europe, is also a first-rate teacher and guide. In addition, his background in literature made him especially appreciative of the problems that arise in trying to put together a piece of work like this. Without Claude, I never would have had the chance to meet the people in the valley, and without that there could have been no book. I am also indebted to Gardner Botsford, of the editorial staff of *The New Yorker*. Writing a long article for that magazine resembled nothing more in my experience than doing a Ph.D. thesis, with the editor in the role of thesis adviser. Gardner Botsford was my thesis adviser, and his numerous suggestions made this a better piece of writing than I could possibly have done on my own. Finally, I am, as always in matters connected with my writing, deeply grateful to William Shawn, the editor of *The New Yorker*. In this case, his enthusiasm for the project and his confidence that it would turn into something gave me the necessary boost whenever I found my own enthusiasm and confidence failing.

PART ONE

Invention

1

The Alternation of Hope and Fear

Alpinism—that is, mountain climbing practiced for its own sake, as a sport—was born in the Chamonix Valley in the latter half of the eighteenth century. At that time, the valley, now part of the Department of the Haute Savoie of France, belonged to the King of Sardinia; in 1858, Napoleon III received Nice and Savoy from the King in return for agreeing to help him drive the Austrians out of Italy, and since March 24, 1860—the Savoyards having ratified the union by a vote of 130,533 to 235—Savoy has belonged to France. In the valley, which was known as Chamouny, the language was a patois French with some overtones of Italian. Today, almost everyone speaks French in the Savoie, although with an accent that must reflect the intonations of the old patois.

The ancient town of Le Prieuré, founded in 1091, has become Chamonix, a sprawling tourist center and, undoubtedly, the mountain-climbing capital of Europe, if not of the world. A visitor to Chamonix, especially during July and August, in the climbing season, finds it difficult to imagine how the old town must have appeared two hundred years ago. Mountains at that time were hated and maligned. Even the names given to them reflected this feeling. For example, one of the satellites of Mont Blanc—which adjoins the valley and is the highest mountain in Europe—is still called Mont Maudit, or Cursed Mountain. An Englishman of that day wrote, "Nature has swept all the *ordures* on Earth into the Alps in order to form and clean the plain of Lombardy," and at the end of the seventeenth century the inhabitants of the valley asked their bishop to come *"exorciser et bénir les montagnes de glace qui menacent la Vallée."* They were not disappointed, and in 1690 they were able to report to the bishop that "since the benediction given by Monseigneur Jean d'Arenthon d'Alex, the glaciers have withdrawn to such an extent that they are at present one-eighth of a league from where they were before his benediction." As a matter of fact, the glaciers are still retreating. As late as 1922, the tip of the Mer de Glace, a glacier that used to flow almost into Chamonix, broke off, and in that spring's floods great blocks of ice were carried into the center of town. Today only the Glacier des Bossons, which flows down from the side of Mont Blanc almost to the floor of the valley in a great cascade of blue-and-white ice, still gives one an impression of menace.

Mountains are now the main business of Chamonix. In the winter, people come from all over the world to ski, and in the summer they come to climb or just look. There are four elaborate systems of *téléphériques* that lead from the valley into the surrounding mountains, and two cog railroads, to say nothing of several lesser ski lifts. One can go from

Chamonix, which is about three thousand feet above sea level, to just below the top of the Aiguille du Midi, which is over twelve thousand feet high, in less than fifteen minutes. The change is stunning. One makes the ascent in two stages. The first *téléphérique* lifts one across a rich pine forest to the timber line, and then above it to the first stop, called the Plan de l'Aiguille. There one changes into a yellow-and-red cabin suspended from a thick metal cable that runs about five thousand feet up an absolutely vertical face. Much of the face is covered with snow and ice, and in the late afternoon, if the weather is warm, it is frequently swept by avalanches. They are a magnificent and awesome sight. There is a roar, and then a thick cloud of snow hurtles down onto the glacier below. Sometimes there are giant cascades of rock, which plow up the snow as they fall. The top of the Aiguille du Midi is a granite pyramid. (Most of the aiguilles—the French word for "needles"—of Chamonix are granite. It provides an excellent surface for climbing, because it is solid and offers a great deal of traction, but it is somewhat dangerous during thunderstorms, since bolts of lightning race unchecked across it.) In the summit pyramid, a system of tunnels has been blasted out. One contains a snack bar and souvenir shop, and another leads to a *téléphérique* that conveys one in little four-man gondolas over the Vallée Blanche, a glacial valley, to the Italian frontier; there one may take another system of *téléphériques* down into Courmayeur, an Italian alpine village and climbing station. From the top of the Aiguille du Midi, one gets an immense feeling of space. On all sides, the snow-covered mountains drop away, and one has the impression of being suspended in midair. As the French climbers put it, *"Il y a du gaz."*

The *téléphérique* to the Aiguille du Midi starts operating at six in the morning. The first couple of runs are devoted to climbers. If the weather is fair, there are usually a few hundred of them assembled around the lower station for the first trip. (The guides estimate that on a good day during the season there are between three and four thousand climbers in the valley.) The rather subdued talk is polyglot, with French predominating. There is a good deal of fussing with equipment and exchanging of information about routes and snow conditions. Here and there one can distinguish guides. Chamonix guides often wear a characteristic red sweater with thin blue stripes, and always wear prominently displayed on their sweaters or jackets a large metal medallion with the initials "S.G.C."—for "Syndicat des Guides de Chamonix"—embossed on its top, just above an impressive enameled depiction of the aiguilles, two crossed ice axes, and the colors of France. At six, the doors of the station are opened, and everyone shoves inside to buy tickets in a wild melee of climbers and equipment. A couple of hours later, the tourists take over—families with large and small children, women who get sick at the top because of the lack of oxygen, and people who insist on going up in thin summer shirts and shorts. There are cameras everywhere. Some people get off at the Plan de l'Aiguille and walk along trails that lead out from the station, but most go on up, take a few pictures, drink a glass of tea, and return to Chamonix. In the village, the same mixture is repeated. There are climbers everywhere. Innumerable sports stores, like La Hutte, sell or rent climbing equipment of every kind. They are set in among souvenir shops, small hotels, and photographers' shops, like Tairraz's. (The Tairraz family has been in mountain photography in Chamonix for over a hundred years.) There are restaurants and cafés and a few *boîtes;* the *Guide Michelin* singles out one of the restaurants, Le Choucas, by crediting it with *"ambiance locale."* The *choucas* is a jet-black mountain jackdaw that, according to local legend, feeds on the remains of expired and expiring climbers. It is one of the few forms of animal life that one sees on and about the really high mountains above Chamonix, and why the restaurant should have picked this somewhat ominous name is not clear, especially since it caters largely to climbers. Almost as incomprehensible is one feature of its décor—a sizable panel of photographs of climbers and skiers who, a guide once told me, "*sont presque tous morts.*"

Until the middle of the eighteenth century, the village was all but unknown, except to a few clergymen, soldiers, and tax collectors. Then, in 1741, a young Englishman named William Windham, who was living in Geneva and becoming bored with it, decided to organize an expedition into the valley. "We left Geneva on the 18th of June, 1741, in a band consisting of eight masters and five servants, all well armed," he later wrote. After three days, they made their way into the valley, which, to their surprise, they found "rather agreeable." They went on to the village of "Chamouny"—Le Prieuré had changed its name. The sight of the glaciers fascinated them. "We camped there, and while refreshments were being prepared for us, we asked the peasants for information about the glaciers," Windham wrote. "First they showed us some of the tips [of the glaciers] which descended into the valley and which we could see from the village. That did not satisfy our curiosity, and we discovered that we had come too far simply to stop. We asked several questions of the peasants in order to find out if by climbing the mountain we could discover something more. They told us that we could but that it was a very difficult and arduous thing to do. One old prior, after a thousand apologies, tried to persuade us not to go any farther. However, our curiosity carried us on."

Windham and his group climbed some steep wooded and rocky slopes above the valley and, after about four hours of very difficult walking, arrived at a spot now known as

Montenvers. Montenvers—the name probably derives from *"montagne verte"*—is a small plateau just above the Mer de Glace. (The ski run from the Aiguille du Midi to below Montenvers by way of the Vallée Blanche and the Mer de Glace is now one of the most famous runs in Europe.) The Mer de Glace has shrunk pitifully since Windham's day. Contemporary etchings and lithographs show it as a tortured river of ice coming almost up to the level of the plain itself. Today, anyone who wants to descend onto the glacier has to use either a little *téléphérique* or a system of extremely steep iron ladders and handrails. Windham's group made what was then the short descent onto the glacier "half falling, half sliding on our hands and feet" and found themselves surrounded by giant ice blocks and crevasses "so deep that we could not even see the bottom." He notes that some of the Chamoniards who came onto the glacier to look for quartz, hematite, and other crystals that are occasionally found there fell into crevasses "and were discovered after some time, their bodies entirely preserved under the ice." After half an hour on the glacier, Windham and his group climbed back up to Montenvers, made their way to Chamouny, and the next day returned to Geneva, their curiosity satisfied.

From Montenvers, which is now easily accessible by an electric cog railway, one gets a clear view of the fantastic architecture of the aiguilles. Stretching southwestward and rising more than five thousand feet above Montenvers is a broken wall of peaks that culminates with the Aiguille du Midi itself. This chain faces directly on the Chamonix Valley, and the mountains that make it up are known collectively as the Aiguilles de Chamonix. In back of them, but invisible from Montenvers, is the Vallée Blanche, which runs east and west, from the Mer de Glace to the base of Mont Blanc itself. From Montenvers, looking due south and up the Mer de

Glace, one can see a second great alpine wall—the one that separates France from Italy. It is dominated by the Grandes Jorasses, which rise to about fourteen thousand feet; the north face of the Grandes Jorasses is one of the most difficult climbs in Chamonix. To the east, directly across the Mer de Glace, is still another chain of aiguilles, this one dominated by the thirteen-thousand-five-hundred-foot Aiguille Verte, which, despite its name, is snow-covered. The whole effect is of wave after wave of mountains, each wave separated from the next by a glacier.

At first glance, the nearby Aiguilles de Chamonix present a totally jumbled arrangement of sharp points (some of the summits are so small that there is barely room for a single climber on them), sawlike ridges, and vertical faces, often seamed with snow. In time, one gets to pick out familiar shapes. There is the Requin (11,224 feet), so called because it resembles a shark's head; the Grépon (11,420), which was thought until the late nineteenth century to be absolutely unclimbable; the Aiguille des Ciseaux (giant granite scissors); the Aiguille du Fou, so called because a well-known guide once said that only a madman would think of climbing it; the Aiguille des Deux Aigles, so called because the first climbers to ascend it (in 1905) were accompanied to the summit by two eagles who flew around and around them. As Windham wrote, these "sharp and arid rocks, elevated to enormous heights, resemble in some way buildings of Gothic architecture." Next to the Aiguille Verte are the twin summits of Les Drus. (The Grand Dru stands at 12,313 feet, and the Petit Dru at 12,245.) The sight of them from Montenvers is one of the most magnificent and awesome alpine scenes in all Europe. The *Guide Vallot*, a four-volume climbing guide that classifies according to difficulty all the climbs in the Chamonix region, says of Les Drus, "*Gigantesque pyramide rocheuse, l'Aiguille du Dru est une des plus pures merveilles*

27

The Aiguille Verte and the Drus. (Courtesy of Bradford Washburn)

de la chaîne du Mont Blanc." Because of their imposing, towering quality, Les Drus have been the subject of innumerable paintings and photographs, and have even figured in novels. In 1964, Gallimard, a French publishing house, brought out a murder mystery by José Giovanni called *Meurte au Sommet*, about a climber who is killed (murder? suicide?) in an avalanche near the summit of Les Drus. The Aiguille Verte, alongside Les Drus, is about twelve hundred feet higher. The top of the Verte is always covered with snow, and it has the reputation of being an especially dangerous mountain to climb. There is a saying in the valley that goes, "*Si la Verte veut, le Mont-Blanc ne peut*"—"If the Verte has decided upon you, Mont Blanc cannot take you." The dangers on the Verte are mainly what climbers call "objective" dangers, meaning those that arise from the condition of the mountain, or perhaps the weather, and are essentially the same for all climbers. On the Verte, the objective dangers are falling rock and avalanches. Many of the routes to the summit involve a climb up exceedingly steep gullies of snow and ice, or at least a traverse across them. These gullies are particularly vulnerable to avalanches. In the summer of 1964, the Verte was the scene of one of the worst accidents that has ever taken place in the Alps. On Tuesday, July 7th, fourteen climbers were killed in a single avalanche. What was even more stunning was that these men were all absolutely crack Alpinists. Nine were students in the French government school in Chamonix—the École Nationale de Ski et d'Alpinisme, sometimes informally known as the Sorbonne de la Neige—which trains guides and ski instructors. They were on a final exercise before being promoted to the rank of full-fledged guide, and were accompanied by four instructors from the school, and also by Charles Bozon, a world-champion skier and former instructor at the school, who had gone along on the climb for the fun of it. The fourteen men were divided up into seven ropes of two each, and had taken a difficult, although often climbed, route. Near the top, they were traversing one of the steep gullies when they were caught in a sudden avalanche that swept them down the gully and onto the glacier below like so many straws. The weather conditions were perfect, and the director of the École Nationale had flown over the mountain in a helicopter just before the climb to make sure that the snow was solid. However, they were surprised by a special type of avalanche known as *une plaque de neige*—a block of snow that peels off for no apparent reason. It is very difficult to spot in advance, and the climbers were simply swept off the mountain. Every precaution had been taken, but the accident occurred anyway. It represented the minimum, ineluctable risk always present in climbing. A guide I spoke with shortly after the accident said simply, "*La montagne, vous savez.*" And Maurice

Herzog, the Annapurna climber who was then the French Secretary of State for Youth and Sports, who came to the funeral as a representative of General de Gaulle, said, "*Je connaissais bien ces garçons; je comprenais bien leur vocation et leur destin.*" Chamonix and all France were stunned by the accident, and for a few days the town practically shut down. But climbers are optimistic by nature, and by the weekend after the accident there was as much activity as ever.

The remarkable change of attitude toward the mountains—from abject fear to an almost lemming-like desire to climb them—was first manifested in Horace-Bénédict de Saussure, a wealthy Genevan who was a geologist and meteorologist of some importance and who became the first of the real mountain climbers and mountain writers. In a book called *Mont-Blanc, Jardin Féerique*, the late Gaston Rébuffat, one of the greatest of the modern Chamonix guides and a prolific mountain writer and photographer, has produced a brilliantly illustrated account of de Saussure's climbs in the Chamonix region. He summarizes de Saussure's contribution to climbing by calling him "the founder of our family." The founder was born near Geneva on February 17, 1740, and fell in love with the mountains in early childhood. He began by making modest climbs near Geneva, and in 1760, "*brulant du désir*" to see the great snow-covered peaks around Chamonix, he made a solo expedition into the valley. His route from Geneva was essentially the same that one would take by automobile now. Mont Blanc is visible from Geneva, but after one leaves the city it is hidden by foothills until one reaches the town of Sallanches, a few miles from the opening of the Chamonix Valley. "From there," de Saussure wrote in his classic *Voyages dans les Alpes*, "it appeared an astonishing height." De Saussure was instantly taken by the valley. He was charmed by everything—"the pure fresh air that one breathes, the beautiful cultivation of the valley, the pretty hamlets that one comes upon at every step." He goes on to say, "The inhabitants give the name '*montagnes maudites*' (cursed mountains) to Mont Blanc and the snow-covered peaks that surround it, and I myself heard from peasants in my infancy that these eternal snows are the result of a curse that the inhabitants of the mountains brought on themselves by their crimes. Until one got to know these good people as one knows them today, this superstitious opinion—absurd as it is—could well have served as a basis for a bad reputation, which was accepted even by people who are ordinarily far above such prejudice." Among the residents of Chamonix, de Saussure discovered a cadre of Chamonix guides. These men were really hunters, and any climbing done by them was done only in the line of duty. De Saussure was much impressed by these men. "What is it that attracts them to this kind of life?" he asks in his book. He was well aware of the extreme dangers of chamois-hunting on the glaciers, and of the numerous accidents that the guides had had. "It is not cupidity," he answers himself, "at least not a rational cupidity, because the most magnificent chamois is not worth more than twelve francs to the man who kills it, even including the value of the meat. . . . It is the danger itself—the alternation of hope and fear, the continual agitation that these emotions make in the soul—that excites the hunter, just as it animates the gambler, the soldier, the navigator, and even, to a point, the Alpine naturalist, whose life resembles in certain respects that of a chamois-hunter." "The alternation of hope and fear," or what a guide once described for me as "*le charme de l'imprévu*," is still as good an explanation as any I know of why men become mountain guides.

De Saussure climbed the Brévent, a pinnacle in the Aiguilles Rouges, across the valley from Mont Blanc (it is

Rébuffat—The art of rock climbing. (Courtesy of P. Tairraz)

now easily accessible by *téléphérique* and is the beginning of one of the most challenging ski runs in the Alps), which affords a superb view of Mont Blanc and the Aiguilles de Chamonix. He was entranced by the view, and Rébuffat writes, "That day—July 24, 1760—is a day of revelation; a great adventure begins. In the heart of a young man, for the first time in the world, there was formed an insane dream. A crazy desire, unreasonable, irrational, was born: to climb Mont Blanc." And in a very real sense, with de Saussure's fantasy the sport of mountaineering began.

Upon descending to the valley, de Saussure announced that he would give a large reward to the first man who found a successful route up Mont Blanc, and that he would even pay daily wages to anyone who *tried* to find one. There were no takers, although one Pierre Simond made a few modest attempts to find the beginnings of a route. (Simond is one of the most common names now found in the valley. There are several Simonds who are guides, and one who is among the world's outstanding manufacturers of mountaineering equipment.) After several years, de Saussure decided that the mountain was unclimbable, and contented himself with making numerous trips around its base.

By 1775, visiting the Chamonix Valley had become almost commonplace. About this time, Marc-Théodore Bourrit, a fellow-townsman of de Saussure's, appeared on the scene. He was almost the perfect anti-type of de Saussure, being poor, uneducated, and physically weak. He felt himself to be greatly inferior to de Saussure, who treated him with disdain. Their only common ground was a mania to climb Mont Blanc; indeed, Bourrit's great ambition was to get to the top before de Saussure. He was a determined, if un-talented, climber, and he did succeed in making a number of lesser climbs (now regarded more or less as hard walks) around the valley. In 1773, he published one of the first books on the valley, *Description des Glacières, Glaciers, et Amas de Glace du Duché de Savoye,* and he became well known in Europe as an alpine painter. In fact, Frederick the Great wrote Bourrit a letter in which he called him "the Historian of the Alps," and in later life Bourrit embellished the gardens of his house in Geneva with, as he put it, "beautiful acacias, planted for the comfort and convenience of strangers who do not wish to leave Geneva without visiting the Historian of the Alps." He also somewhat later succeeded—with at least the tacit aid of de Saussure—in writing and publicizing an entirely distorted and dishonest version of the first ascent of Mont Blanc, which was taken at face value until the middle of the nineteenth century.

The first real attempt on the mountain was made in 1775. Four Chamonix guides, carrying, among other things, long lances, which they used as supports in traversing crevasses, managed to get to the top (14,120 feet) of the Dôme du Goûter—a rounded summit only sixteen hundred feet below the peak of Mont Blanc and now on the most frequently used route to it. Before they could reach the top of Mont Blanc, thick clouds began forming, and they retreated back to the valley. They had counted on making the whole climb in one day, because it was universally held at the time that no one could spend a night on the glaciers and survive. (Today, very few people would think of climbing Mont Blanc in one day.) Several years went by before the next serious attempt, and this time there was a new figure on the scene—Dr. Michel-Gabriel Paccard, a young physician, born in Chamonix in 1757, who had studied medicine in Turin and Paris, and had returned to Chamonix to settle down and practice. In 1784, after making an unsuccessful attempt on the Dôme du Goûter side of the mountain in the company of none other than Bourrit and some guides (Bourrit became terrified because of a turn of bad weather, and the attempt was aborted), Dr. Paccard began a serious telescopic study of the mountain, and hit upon a new idea. Until then, the climb had begun from the Chamonix side; now Paccard decided that it would be easier to start farther down the valley, first climbing to the Tête Rousse, then the Aiguille du Goûter, then the Dôme du Goûter, and finally to the summit itself. Late in the summer of 1784, Paccard explored the new route, and in September Bourrit and some guides tried it. Bourrit was stopped below the summit of the Aiguille du Goûter, but two of his guides made it to the top and continued to the top of the Dôme, where they were finally stopped by the difficulty of the summit ridge. (Today, the so-called *voie normale* up Mont Blanc follows Paccard's plan. One begins in Saint-Gervais, a small town just outside the Chamonix Valley, where one boards a cog railroad that goes as far as the Nid d'Aigle, at about eight thousand feet. Here there is a small railroad station and buffet, and close by, on a cliff where one begins the climb to the summit, a sign reading, "Mt. Blanc: 8h"—eight hours, broken into two days, with a stopover in a mountain refuge, being about the standard time for the climb.) As a result of the success of his guides, Bourrit proposed to de Saussure that they make a joint try at the mountain. Rébuffat quotes de Saussure's answer: "I always prefer to go on excursions of this type alone with my guides, but I will consent with pleasure." In September, 1785, de Saussure, Bourrit, Bourrit's son Isaac, and fourteen guides proceeded to a cabin that Bourrit had had constructed at the foot of the Aiguille du Goûter. It may well have been the first climbing hut ever built; now there are no fewer than three mountain refuges between the Nid d'Aigle and the summit, and several more on the other approaches to it. On this trip, de Saussure made frequent use of an extraordinary climbing technique that he had developed on earlier expeditions. It consisted of stationing one guide in

35

front of him and one behind him, each holding one end of a long climbing baton, to which de Saussure, in the middle, was able to cling. But the technique did not always work. "Often, not knowing what else to hold on to, I was reduced to seizing the bottom of the foot of the guide who was in front of me," he wrote later.

The caravan never got to the top of the Aiguille du Goûter and was fortunate to get back unscathed to Chamonix. A totally absurd altercation followed, which is wonderfully described in a book by Sir Arnold Lunn entitled *The Swiss and Their Mountains*. As Sir Arnold tells it, "De Saussure, on his return to Geneva, was annoyed by reports which not only greatly exaggerated the perils which they had encountered but which also attributed the failure of the expedition to his shortcomings as a rock climber. To his protest, Bourrit replied, 'I could not but notice that the way you came down was not the happiest. You might have fallen backwards, you might have been hit by the rocks dislodged by the guides, whom you made keep behind you, and we noticed the trouble they had to avoid this.' " To atone for this attack, the Historian later sent de Saussure an account of the expedition (which he no doubt intended to publish) that praised him in overelaborate terms. De Saussure found this excessive praise even less to his taste than the unjustified criticism. "No one, perhaps," he magnanimously wrote in a return letter, "believes more than I do in the kindness and honesty of your heart, but I know very well also that your flighty imagination often makes you see things in a false light. If you could put aside this tendency, there is no reason you should not keep an agreeable recollection of our excursion. I had every reason to be satisfied with you and your son." Meanwhile, the son had himself launched an attack on de Saussure in a vainglorious letter. "Sir," he wrote, "do you not envy me my twenty-one years? Who will wonder if a youth

Jacques Balmat.
(Courtesy of Gaston
Rébuffat)

of this age, who has nothing to lose, is bolder than a father of
a family, a man of forty-six?" As Lunn goes on to say, "Even
this impudent letter could only provoke a gentle retort: 'A
moderate amount of boastfulness is no great crime, especially at your age. . . . One may proclaim oneself a little
stronger, a little more active than one really is, and yet be the
most honest fellow in the world. The truth is that though I
recognized in you a slight tendency in this direction, I did
not fail to find you very amiable.' "

However, de Saussure, although he treats the Bourrits
very well in his *Voyages,* refused to climb with them again,
and the elder Bourrit's last attempt on Mont Blanc, in 1788,
ended in failure about four hundred feet below the summit.
As for Paccard, he and de Saussure had some correspon-
dence about their respective attempts on the Aiguille du

Goûter in which de Saussure more or less dismissed Paccard's achievements. Neither de Saussure nor Bourrit could accept the fact that a humble village doctor, almost singlehanded and without a vast retinue of guides and servants, could do as well or better than they.

Now still another new figure enters the drama—Jacques Balmat. Balmat was a Chamoniard guide and hunter, and his principal motive for climbing was a desire to earn the prize that de Saussure had offered nearly thirty years before. In 1786, Balmat made an attempt on the summit with a number of fellow-guides. They were turned back by a storm, and Balmat, losing the rest of the party, was forced to spend a night at more than twelve thousand feet—probably the first bivouac ever attempted at such an altitude. At this point, the myth about the first climb of Mont Blanc begins. De Saussure writes in his *Voyages* that Balmat, while resting

M. G. Paccard.
(Courtesy of Gaston
Rébuffat)

in his bivouac and contemplating the mountain, spotted a new route to the summit from the Chamonix side. He planned to keep it secret but then, hearing that Dr. Paccard was ready to make another attempt, he offered his services (and, according to the myth, his route) to him for hire. In reality, it appears that the route the two men finally took was Dr. Paccard's own, which he had plotted out as a result of very careful telescopic observations of the mountain, and which was quite unknown to Balmat before the climb. In any event, on Monday, August 7, 1786, the two men started up, Balmat carrying most of the provisions, which included a barometer that Paccard made frequent use of to check his altitude. On the night of August 7th, which was exceptionally warm, they bivouacked at 7,640 feet. At four the next morning, they started up again. Sir Arnold Lunn notes, "On no less than four occasions, [they] broke through small concealed crevasses and saved themselves by flinging themselves forward, with poles horizontal, to the snow. They had no rope. At some point above the Grands Mulets, Balmat felt that he had had enough. [The Grands Mulets is a rock outcropping above the glaciers, on which there is now a very elaborate mountain refuge.] He told Paccard that his child was ill and that he had promised to return to help his wife. Paccard dismissed the story of the sick child as a mere excuse, though in fact the child was ill and had died before they returned to Chamonix. . . . There was a second crisis when they reached the Grand Plateau. Once again, Balmat refused to continue. They had been climbing for nine hours. The wind had risen, the temperature had fallen, and there was no certainty that they would reach the summit before sunset. Paccard's decision to continue was outstandingly courageous. We can understand Balmat's misgivings, and must give him full credit for overcoming his natural reluctance to continue. They were observed from the valley to leave the Petits Mulets rocks at 6:12 P.M. and to reach the summit at 6:23 P.M. on August 8, 1786."

The route they took is by no means the easiest one, and few climbers would like to be on the summit as late as 7 P.M., which is when Balmat and Paccard began their descent to Chamonix. The whole ascent had been witnessed by a Baron Adolf von Gersdorf through a high-powered telescope and carefully recorded by him in a journal. This was fortunate for Paccard's subsequent reputation, because no sooner had the climbers returned to Chamonix than Bourrit put all his energies to work to discredit Dr. Paccard. He created the story that Paccard had been all but carried to the top by Balmat (in fact, Paccard did become snow-blind on the way down, and was partly led by Balmat), and that Balmat had discovered the route that the climbers used. Balmat—who received de Saussure's prize, amounting to about sixty dollars, plus his guide's fee and the right, conferred on him by the King of Sardinia, to sign his name "Jacques Balmat, dit Mont-Blanc"—went as far as to sign an affidavit attesting to Dr. Paccard's crucial role in the climb. But it appears to have been ignored, and Bourrit succeeded in discrediting Paccard to such an extent that when the Doctor wrote an account of the climb, he could never get it printed. In a brief introduction to a masterly historical study called *The First Ascent of Mont Blanc*, by T. Graham Brown and Sir Gavin de Beer, Sir John Hunt, the leader of the successful British Everest expedition, writes, "Reading the long accepted myth of Dr. Paccard being supported by his companion Balmat to the highest point after the latter had returned from the top to fetch him, I was reminded of the illustrations of an unconscious Hillary being dragged hand over hand to the summit of Everest by conquering Tenzing (who had no such notion), which adorned the triumphal arches along the road as we returned to Kathmandu. . . .

Incident before reaching the Grand Mulets—Grand Mulets in the center distance. (From *Ten Scenes in the Last Ascent of Mont Blanc* by J. D. H. Brown, 1853.)

Thus lesser men will ever seek their own advantage, even from adventure in high places."

As part of his campaign, Bourrit wrote a vicious pamphlet attacking Paccard, which was published in Geneva. De Saussure, who knew the truth and could have set the record straight, saw the pamphlet but did essentially nothing about it. Thus, the legend denying Paccard's achievement grew, and it was perpetuated by no less a figure than Alexandre Dumas *père*, who visited Chamonix in 1832 and interviewed Balmat. By this time, Balmat, who appears to have been something of a moral coward, had changed his story, even claiming that the original affidavit was a forgery. Dumas had no knowledge of alpine climbing, but he had a well-developed view that all guides were supermen. Balmat, liberally plied with wine and under no inhibitions about failing to tell the truth, since all the principals were now dead— Paccard in 1827 and Bourrit in 1819—produced a bold and almost completely untrue version of the ascent, which Dumas took at face value. The interview was printed and reprinted in many languages, and the legend was taken to be historical fact. Its debunking, which is described in great detail by Brown and de Beer, seems to have had its origin in the publication of a diary of the English climber Gilbert Elliot, Earl of Minto, which was published in 1892. He had been on an expedition near Zermatt in 1830 with Ambroise Paccard, the Doctor's son, who informed Lord Minto that his father had been slighted in the history of the climb, and that he had documents to prove it, including a copy of Balmat's affidavit. Lord Minto's reference to this long-forgotten affidavit caught the eye of a number of British climbers who read his diary and decided to investigate further. In 1909, H. F. Montagnier, a Swiss mountaineer; Edward Whymper, the first man to climb the Matterhorn; and Dr. Heinrich Dübi, a Swiss climber and well-known editor of Alpine guidebooks, met in Geneva to plan a concerted attempt to learn the real history of the first climb of Mont Blanc. Soon after this meeting, Montagnier turned up a copy of the prospectus that Paccard had written in an attempt to sell his planned book, and although it was badly nibbled by mice, it disclosed the fact that one Baron von Gersdorf headed the list of subscribers to the book. This led to Dübi's discovery of von Gersdorf's eyewitness account of the whole ascent as he had seen it through a telescope from Chamonix. In addition, Montagnier managed to find in de Saussure's journal, which was in the possession of de Saussure's grandson, the transcript of a long interview that de Saussure had had with Paccard just after the climb. As a final step, de Beer discovered in 1955 a careful description of the climb in Dr. Paccard's own hand, including the various barometric readings he had taken along the route to determine the altitudes. The combined evidence of these documents provides a convincing picture of what actually happened on the climb, and enables one to follow it step by step. But all this is of recent vintage; a hundred years ago it was even being claimed in some books that de Saussure was the first man to climb Mont Blanc.

As it happened, in 1787, at the age of forty-seven, de Saussure did succeed in making the third ascent of the mountain, which had been climbed in between by Balmat and two other guides. De Saussure took with him a servant and eighteen guides, including Balmat, and among the bits of personal equipment that were carried up for him were a table of logarithms, two half bottles of *eau de cerises*, mattresses, bed linen and a green curtain, two green jackets, a white suit and three vests, five pairs of shoes, five shirts for day wear and four to be worn at night, stockings of silk and wool, six half bottles of white wine, and a parasol. The party had a tent, and a stepladder for crossing crevasses. Rébuffat, in his book, has some splendid etchings, done by Marquart Wocher, a well-known Swiss mountain artist of the early nineteenth century, that show this improbable caravan plodding its way across the glaciers. One of the most interesting features of the etchings is some retouching that de Saussure ordered before publication was allowed. The original shows de Saussure as a portly middle-aged gentleman sliding down a glacial slope on his backside while two guides appear to be struggling to make sure he doesn't fall into a crevasse. In the retouched version, he has lost several pounds and many years, and is shown striding along the glaciers with the regal, commanding air of a prince. At the summit, de Saussure made numerous scientific observations, and at one-thirty in the afternoon the party began its long and triumphal descent to the valley. "I spent the next day at Chamouni to make some comparative observations," de Saussure wrote, "after which we returned completely happy to Geneva, from where I see Mont Blanc with real pleasure and without feeling that sentiment of trouble and pain that it used to cause me." Balmat, perhaps ironically, had lost his life in the mountains in 1834 while searching for a vein of gold.

It was not long before Chamonix became the new mode. Hotels were built, and people came from all over Europe to see the mountains and, in some cases, to try to climb them. In 1808, the first woman—Marie Paradis, a native of the valley—climbed Mont Blanc. Her brief, very frank account of the experience is one of the delights of mountain literature: "I was at my work when the guides, conducted by Jacques Balmat, who were just leaving for Mont Blanc, came up to say to me, 'Marie, you are a nice girl who needs to earn her living. Come with us. We will take you to the summit, and afterward foreigners will want to come and look at you and give you presents.' That decided me, and I left with them. At the Grand Plateau, I couldn't go any farther. . . . I was really sick. . . . I lay down on the snow. I puffed like a chicken that is too hot. They took me by both arms and pulled me, but at the Rochers Rouges I found it impossible to go on." And then comes, in the patois of Savoy, a touching lament that probably would sound quite familiar to any modern Chamonix guide. Said Marie, *"Ficha mé din una crevasse et alla ô vo vodra"*—"Dump me in a crevasse and go wherever you want." (Armand Charlet, who was generally acknowledged to be the greatest of the prewar Chamonix guides, once told me about a lady client of his whom he took from Chamonix to Zermatt, in Switzerland, via the Haute Route, across the glaciers. The Haute Route usually takes about five days, either on foot or on skis; huts are situated along the route about one day's march apart. At the end of the fourth day, Charlet's client was tiring, but Charlet had hopes that the sight of the Matterhorn, near Zermatt, would revive her. However, when she finally saw the great peak, she lay down in the snow and said, "I have now seen the Matterhorn, and I want to stay here and die." Charlet told her, in no uncertain terms, that he did not intend to die watching the Matterhorn, and managed to persuade her to go on to Zermatt.) Marie continues, "The guides responded by saying, 'It is necessary that you go on to the top.' They took me, they pulled me, they pushed me, and finally we got there." Upon being asked what she had seen from the summit, Marie said, "On the summit I could not see clearly; I could neither breathe nor talk. It was very white where I was, and very dark wherever else I looked."

Between 1786 and 1850, there were thirty-nine successful climbs of Mont Blanc, including the second climb by a woman—the Countess Henriette d'Angeville, who made the ascent in 1838 with a caravan that rivaled de Saussure's. She became known as the Fiancée du Mont Blanc, and her costume, which included fur gloves and a boa, was frequently sketched by contemporary artists. Near the summit, in a state of extreme exhaustion, she told the guides, "If I die before getting to the top, drag my body up and leave it there; my family will reward you for carrying out my last wishes." However, she did get to the top, and there released a pigeon with a note tied to its foot reading, "At 1:25, Mlle. d'Angeville arrived at the summit of Mont Blanc, along with the eight people who accompanied her." The unfortunate pigeon landed in the nearby village of Les Contamines, where it was shot on the roof of the church and eaten by the curé; its identity was established by the string that was still tied to its foot. By this time, the now standard route to the summit—via Saint-Gervais and the Nid d'Aigle—had become popular. In 1819, Joseph-Nicolas Genoux-Roux, the proprietor of a hotel near Saint-Gervais, distributed a number of advertising placards announcing his readiness to organize guided trips to the summit by the new route. "If the traveller cannot get to the summit of Mont Blanc because of a lack of intelligence, discouragement, or any other reason that is the fault of the guides, the guides will receive no salary," his proposal went. "Exceptions to this condition are bad weather, discouragement, and any other indispositions on the part of the traveller—in a word, all obstacles that are not part of the guide's function." Genoux-Roux insisted that four guides were absolutely necessary for one climber but that five could take two climbers. Each guide was to receive twenty-five francs (about five dollars) in addition to his food. (In 1964, a climb of Mont Blanc by the standard route cost two hundred and seventy-four new francs—almost exactly the amount of de Saussure's prize—in guide's fees, plus food and lodging and the cost of whatever lifts or trains are used. A guide will take two, or sometimes three, climbers on one rope.)

By the early eighteen-twenties, society had come to Chamonix, and a writer noted in 1823, "Never has nature been more in fashion, nor fashion closer to nature. Women dressed in decorated dresses, English ladies in travelling dresses richly embroidered, men in black suits and *en grande tenue*—such is the spectacle that the Auberge de l'Union offers us. A dinner with sixty places is served, and some of the ladies, while waiting for it to be ready, play the piano, while others rest in the corner near the fire. . . . M. Charlet, who is the *aubergiste*, comes and goes, and animates his waiters with his voice, gestures, and looks; there isn't more activity on a boat during a storm."

On May 9, 1823, the King of Sardinia issued a decree proclaiming the founding of the Syndicat des Guides de Chamonix. The decree consisted of fifty-eight articles, and began, "There shall be formed in the Commune of Chamonix a company of guides designated to conduct and direct, both on the glaciers and anywhere else, foreigners who have need of them while visiting the Valley of Chamonix." The decree contained a long list of the guides' functions and obligations, even down to the training of the young. "On ordinary climbs, the guides may take with them their children or other young people of the valley, in order that they may one day join the Company; however, the guides may do this the first time only after obtaining the consent of the 'Chef des Guides,' and . . . these young people may never be counted as guides, nor can they in any way be put in charge of travellers." At the same time, a fund for aiding the families of guides who had been killed or disabled while climbing was established. It was, and is, financed largely by the "*masse*," a kind of informal fund into which each guide pays a fixed percentage—five per cent in Chamonix now—of his fees. At first, the number of guides in the Syndicat was limited to forty, but in 1846 it was increased to sixty, and in 1852 was made unlimited. Until the early nineteen-thirties, no one who was not born in or near Chamonix (within about ten kilometers) could be a Chamonix guide. The first outsider to be admitted to the Syndicat was Roger Frison-Roche, but even he, though born in Paris, was of Chamonix stock and at seventeen had come back to live in the valley. He is one of the foremost mountain writers in the world, his best-known novel, *Premier de Cordée*, dealing with the education of a young Chamonix guide.

Although the climb of Mont Blanc had become fairly common by the time of the founding of the Syndicat, none of the other peaks in the valley—with one remarkable exception—had received any attention from climbers. The exception was the Aiguille du Midi, which hovers like a fantastic vertical wall over Chamonix. From the Chamonix side, the Aiguille is still considered a difficult climb, but when it is approached from the back, up the Mer de Glace and the Vallée Blanche, it is relatively easy. The first person to climb the Aiguille was a mysterious and romantic Polish count named Antoni Malczewski, said to have been *"beau et séduisant"* and the idol of the salons of Warsaw. The Count arrived in Chamonix in the summer of 1818, when he was twenty-five, and decided to climb the Aiguille du Midi because it had never been done. He engaged a party of guides and set off up the Mer de Glace. After a short night's sleep near the head of the Mer, the Count and his party began the ascent of the Vallée Blanche. At four in the afternoon, after a twelve-hour climb, they reached the northern summit of the Aiguille. Count Malczewski had the idea of going on, by a long and difficult traverse, to the summit of Mont Blanc itself, but his party was not equipped to spend the night on the snow, so he returned to the valley and climbed Mont Blanc a few days later—"a pleasure in comparison with the sad and terrible Aiguille du Midi." It was his last climb. He returned to Warsaw and died there eight years later, in a "mixture of mystical crises, of a veritable delirium both spiritual and sentimental," according to a contemporary account. Moreover, his ascent of the Aiguille was completely forgotten. In fact, almost forty years later, when Count Fernand de Bouillé and ten guides reached the central summit of the Aiguille—or, more precisely, when two of de Bouillé's guides, Alexandre Devouassoud and Ambroise Simond, reached the central summit—they were under the impression that no one had been there before. De Bouillé, who was opposed to Napoleon III and wanted a restoration of the monarchy in France, intended to make the climb for the sole purpose of planting the royal flag where no flag had ever stood, as an affront to the Emperor. The group left Chamonix in an atmosphere of drama and apprehension. Tourists sadly shook de Bouillé's hand in farewell, and an ancient guide told the party, "My poor friends, you would do very well to stay home; Jacques Balmat could never climb it, and you won't get any further than he did." The group followed the route of the forgotten Malczewski and spent the night on the Vallée Blanche. There was a good deal of the atmosphere of a picnic about the whole thing. Everyone had brought along plenty to drink, and there was singing and general merriment until midnight, when the weather became almost unbearably cold. A little before four o'clock, the party got under way again, and, after hours of severe effort, came within several meters of the summit. The place where they stopped was the target of small avalanches of stones and ice, and Ambroise Simond told de Bouillé to take shelter while he and Devouassoud tried to fight their way to the summit. The Count agreed, and an hour later the two guides came back, pale and trembling. "*Monsieur le comte, votre drapeau flotte là-haut*," said Devouassoud, adding, "The climb is

49

done, but all the money in the world would not get me to do it again." Simond agreed. "Perhaps my soul will go there again after I die, but my body—never!" he said. Upon returning to Chamonix, the Count and his party were greeted by a crowd of fifteen hundred people. An arch of triumph had been erected in front of his hotel, and when the Count passed beneath it, he was given a crown and a certificate from the chief of guides attesting to his having made the first ascent of "the terrible Aiguille." Speaking of the harrowing climb, de Bouillé said, "I doubt if there will ever be a second."

Construction of the comfortable *téléphérique* that runs up the Chamonix face of the Aiguille du Midi began in 1949,

Téléphérique of the Aiguille du Midi. (Courtesy of P. Tairraz)

under the direction of the brilliant Italian engineer Dino Lora-Totino. A caravan of thirty guides, some from Chamonix, and some from the Italian side of Mont Blanc, carried a steel cable—seventeen hundred meters long, and weighing nearly twenty-five hundred pounds—up the route followed by Malczewski, de Bouillé, and innumerable climbers since. The guides were about ten feet apart, and each man carried some seventy pounds of cable. On July 29, 1949, the cable was lowered along the north face, toward Chamonix; three French and three Italian guides were attached to its end, in order to keep it from catching on the rocks. This cable served as the basis for the construction of the *téléphérique*, which went into service in 1954. In 1960 alone, five hundred thousand people were transported to the top. Since 1959, when I first visited the valley, I have ridden up on the *téléphérique* many times—early in the morning and at sunset, in fog, in snow, and in thunderstorms, when there were temporary power failures. I have mixed feelings about it. On the one hand, it brings thousands of people into the heart of the high mountains, which they would otherwise never see; on the other, it mars what is otherwise an absolutely primitive and forbidding landscape. At night, one can see the lights of the top *téléphérique* station glittering down on Chamonix almost like the jewels in a crown. It is a lovely and friendly sight, and one cannot help thinking back to the early Chamonix guides and their clients, who had the courage, for whatever reasons, to reach up to where no one had been before them.

2

Whymper and Mummery

It has often been said that the British invented mountain climbing. This is not really so if one means that the British were the first to conceive the idea of climbing mountains for some reason other than military strategy or commercial transport. (As far as anyone knows, the first European to announce publicly that his goal was to get to the top of a snow-covered mountain more or less just for the sake of getting there was de Saussure.) What the British *did* do was to make mountain climbing a sport. Most of the early climbing expeditions were just that—expeditions. A climb of Mont Blanc usually involved a whole caravan of people, mostly porters carrying all sorts of luxuries to the top so that the climber—generally a wealthy aristocrat—would not miss the comforts of home. A successful ascent of Mont Blanc was always followed by a cannonade, and sometimes by fireworks, in the valley. Between 1786 and 1829, there were only nineteen recorded climbs of Mont Blanc, but between 1829 and 1856 there were seventy-five. (By now, the number has reached the tens of thousands, and the returning climber, unless he has taken a tremendously difficult route or had an accident, is completely unnoticed among the hordes of climbers in the valley.) Before 1850, the British had done no significant climbing in the Alps. In his book on the history of alpine mountaineering, *The Swiss and Their Mountains,* Sir Arnold Lunn has compiled a kind of scorecard by nationality of climbing prior to 1850. He finds that the Swiss have the most impressive record, followed by the French and the Italians; the English are almost unrepresented. A decade later, however, the Alps had become an English playground. Indeed, in a book entitled *The Alps in Nature and History,* W. A. B. Coolidge, a well-known late-nineteenth-century climber and alpine traveler, remarks, "Whereas from 1787 to 1850 there had been only seventeen English . . . ascents of Mont Blanc to sixteen non-English, travelers of no nationality other than English or American (eleven of these only) made the ascent of Mont Blanc in 1850, 1851, 1852, 1853 and 1855." And Sir Arnold sums it all up by saying, "Within a few years [of 1850], the initiative had passed from the Swiss to the British. In the Golden Age of mountaineering, which ended with the first ascent of the Matterhorn, in 1865, of the thirty-nine major peaks first ascended during this period, no less than thirty-one were first ascended by British amateurs, most of whom were, of course, accompanied by Swiss guides." In 1857, the British founded the Alpine Club, the first such mountaineering organization, and in 1863 the club published the first issue of the *Alpine Journal,* the world's oldest mountaineering paper. In the same year, John Ball's

Guide to the Western Alps, the first climbing guide, was published.

A combination of factors seems to have contributed to the change. For one, the increasing prosperity of the Victorian era had given rise to an English leisure class that had the time, the inclination, and the organization for sports and adventure. Sir Arnold puts it this way: "The fact that it was the British who founded the first Alpine Club is not altogether surprising. Man has been defined as a tool-making animal, and an Englishman might be defined as a club-making animal. The first thing the British did after establishing a base in some remote African or Asiatic colony was to found a club. The organization of sport in 1850 was more developed in Great Britain than in any other country." De Saussure's *Voyages dans les Alpes*, published in 1779, was widely read in England, and it did much to bring Englishmen to Chamonix and elsewhere in the Alps. One of the first, and most influential, people to heed de Saussure's call was John Ruskin, who read the *Voyages* in 1833, at the age of fourteen. He was struck by the illustrations, and persuaded his parents to take him to the valley to see if there really were objects as fantastic as those described by de Saussure. He was thunderstruck by what he saw. It was not only Mont Blanc that impressed him but all of the Aiguilles. They had frequently reminded people of the spires of Gothic cathedrals, and, indeed, Ruskin built an entire religious mystique upon the valley and its peaks. He contemplated the Aiguilles for hours, frequently from the base of the Brévent, a pinnacle across the valley from Chamonix. The mountains, he wrote, "seem to have been built for the human race as at once their schools and cathedrals—full of treasures of illuminated manuscript for the scholar, kindly in simple lessons for the worker, quiet in pale cloisters for the thinker, glorious in holiness for the worshipper." And he drew some of the most beautiful and precise sketches ever done of the Chamonix region. Under the title *Of Mountain Beauty,* these are included in his collection *Modern Painters.* Here one finds the first pictures of the Aiguilles in which all the details recognizably correspond to what one sees today. The earlier artists had brought a wonderful sense of fantasy to their work, making the region look like a corner of Dante's Inferno, with climbers usually shown bravely hanging on to absolutely vertical walls over the incalculable abyss.

Ruskin was not a climber. In fact, as far as is known, he made only one attempt, and that an abortive one, on a modest peak in the Aiguilles Rouges—the collection of smaller but very beautiful mountains across the valley from the Mont Blanc massif. Eventually, Ruskin came to hate the British climbers who swarmed into the valley to "defile" his "Temple of Nature." "I would that the enlightened population of Paris and London were content with doing nothing—that they were satisfied with expenditure upon their idle pleasures in their idle way," he wrote in *Modern Painters,* adding, "The valley of Chamouni . . . is rapidly being turned into a kind of Cremorne Gardens."

Another figure who publicized Chamonix and the Alps for the English was almost equally curious. He was Albert Smith, an English journalist, who climbed Mont Blanc in 1851. His climb appears to have been quite uneventful, but he shrewdly conceived the idea that he could make money from it by telling about it—with a few spectacular exaggerations—in public. Accordingly, on March 15, 1852, he hired the Egyptian Hall, in London, and delivered an illustrated lecture on his climb. Smith's pictures were appropriately hair-raising, and they were later assembled into a game called "The Ascent of Mont Blanc," in which the players proceed in fifty steps from "the South Eastern Terminus"—the departure for Dover—to the summit, nego-

A. F. Mummery.
(Courtesy of Gaston
Rébuffat)

tiating such intervening obstacles as "A Sick Traveller," "Soft
Snow," and "Travellers Lose Their Footing." The lectures and
the game had considerable success, and eventually Smith
was invited to Windsor Castle to present his program before
Queen Victoria. He subsequently modified the program to
include music and an appearance by his guide, François
Favret, along with some St. Bernard dogs.

Whether because of Smith's influence or not, 1854 is generally recognized as the year in which the British first came to
the Alps in force. The story of British alpine climbing is very
long and complicated, but its two most important moments
are the climbing of the Matterhorn (14,780 feet) by Edward
Whymper in 1865 and the climbing of the Grépon (11,420
feet) by A. F. Mummery in 1881. The two mountains are

Edward Whymper.
(Courtesy of Boissonnas,
Geneva)

completely dissimilar. The Matterhorn stands almost isolated on the Swiss-Italian border above Zermatt. It is a
formidable-looking mountain, and before the middle of the
nineteenth century it was thought to be unclimbable. However, Whymper finally discovered a route that made it a
comparatively easy climb; in the years since, with the aid of
fixed cables near the top, thousands of climbers, many of
them with little or no prior experience, have followed
Whymper's route, and the local guides have been heard to
express confidence that they could get a cow to the top. As
for the Grépon, near Chamonix, it is bunched in together
with its neighboring aiguilles and does not stand out notably when seen from the valley. The Grépon is the perfect
abstraction of a Chamonix aiguille, having almost vertical
walls broken by thin cracks, which divide its faces into

enormous parallelepipeds, and climbing it is by most standards an extremely acrobatic feat, requiring a good deal of technical skill. Before Mummery's ascent, it, too, was universally held to be impossible.

The story of Whymper's climb of the Matterhorn has been told many times—most graphically in his own *Scrambles Amongst the Alps*, written in 1871. *Scrambles* is not only a classic of mountaineering literature but one of the most delightful and moving adventure books ever written. It begins with Whymper's first trip to the Continent, in 1860, and ends with his climb of the Matterhorn in 1865. Reading between the lines, one can get some idea of the man who wrote it, but a clearer portrait appears in a 1940 book entitled *Edward Whymper,* by the great English Himalayan climber Francis Smythe. Whymper was born in London in 1840 and, after a few years of schooling, was apprenticed to his father's engraving business. At fifteen, he began a meticulous diary, which he kept throughout his life. Reading its early sections (quoted at some length by Smythe) is something of a shock—"a strangely depressing experience," as Smythe puts it, explaining, "It is the story of a boy of quick intelligence and high ambition tied down to dull and monotonous work." The diary is filled with entries like "Jan. 29, 1856: Murders are plentiful about this time of year; there have been several fresh ones lately. Very cold and dry." There is no intimation of the future Whymper except in a striking entry dated June 4, 1858: "In evening, I visited for the first time Mr. Albert Smith's entertainment of Mont Blanc etc., which closes this season finally, previous to Mr. Smith going to China for a new entertainment. People often go to these sorts of things with exorbitant expectations raised by previous descriptions which have told them; I, however, found myself quite satisfied and more."

By this time, Whymper had something of a reputation as

a watercolorist, and in 1860 the English publisher William Longman, wanting some alpine illustrations for a book he was bringing out, commissioned him to go to the Continent to make them. He left England in July and traveled all through the Alps, coming late in the summer to Zermatt and the Matterhorn. Smythe quotes from the entries he made in his diary at this time: "Saw of course the Matterhorn repeatedly; what precious stuff Ruskin has written about this, as well as about many other things. When one has a fair view of the mountain, as I had, it may be compared to a sugar loaf set up on a table; the sugar loaf should have its head knocked on one side. Grand it is, but beautiful I think it is not." He began his climbing career in Zermatt with walks on the glaciers—sometimes by himself, sometimes with other English climbers, and sometimes with local peasants who hired themselves out as guides to supplement their incomes. (This is still true of many of the older generation of guides, even in Chamonix, where guiding has been an organized profession since 1823.) The illustrations were apparently a success, for the next year Whymper was back in the Alps with another commission from Longman. This time, Longman was especially interested in sketches of the Dauphiné Alps, a wild and primitive part of France not far from Grenoble and at this time largely unexplored. Here, with a small group, including an ancient and totally incompetent local guide, Whymper made the first ascent of Mont Pelvoux, which is 12,973 feet high. It was his initial first ascent. Up to this time, Smythe notes, "Whymper had a poor opinion of Alpine guides; they seemed to him little more than 'pointers out of paths and large consumers of meat and drink.' " However, at this juncture in his life he met the first of the two guides who were to share so much of his future destiny—Jean-Antoine Carrel, of Valtournanche, on the Italian side of the Matterhorn. (The second was Michel Croz, of Chamonix.) Carrel was the first guide who felt that the Matterhorn could be climbed, and—what was more important to him, since he was a fervent patriot—he felt that it could be climbed from the Italian side. "He was the only man who persistently refused to accept defeat and who continued to believe, in spite of all discouragements, that the great mountain was not inaccessible," Whymper writes in *Scrambles*. In August of 1861, with Carrel and an uncle of his, J.-J. Carrel, Whymper made his first attempt on the Matterhorn. They were turned back, but the experience made Whymper resolve to keep at the Matterhorn "until one or the other was vanquished."

The following year, Whymper was back. During the previous winter, he had spent much time designing climbing equipment—something that became a lifelong concern of his—and had devised for high altitudes a compact bivouac tent that was the forerunner of the modern lightweight climbing tent. (He also designed a kind of metal "claw" for gripping difficult rock.) When he returned to Valtournanche in the summer, he engaged as a porter a remarkably courageous and devoted hunchback named Luc Meynet. Meynet, who was a cheesemaker by trade, had a completely spontaneous love of the mountains. Of one of their attempts on the Matterhorn, Whymper writes, "I proposed to the hunchback to accompany me alone, to see if we could not get higher than before, though of reaching the summit there was little or no hope. He did not hesitate, and in a few hours we stood—for the third time together—upon the Col du Lion, but it was the first time Meynet had seen the view unclouded. The poor little deformed peasant gazed upon it silently and reverently for a time and then unconsciously fell on one knee in an attitude of adoration and clasped his hands, exclaiming in ecstasy, 'O beautiful mountains!' His actions were as appropriate as his words were natural, and tears bore witness to the reality of his emotion."

By the end of 1864, Whymper had made six attempts on

Michel Croz. (Courtesy
of Emile Gos)

the Matterhorn, including one desperate solo climb during
which he had a fall that left him with a scar on the side of his
head. (In a curious footnote in *Scrambles,* he describes the fall
as being almost pleasant, and concludes that "death by a fall
from a great height is as painless an end as can be experienced.") Carrel had also been active on the mountain, with
other English climbers, but no one had come near to forcing
the summit. Whymper described himself as "defeated and
disconsolate, but, like a gambler who loses each throw, only
the more eager to have another try." It was at this time that he
began his association with Michel Croz, whom many people
consider the greatest of the nineteenth-century Chamonix
guides. An English climber who had climbed with Croz in
the Dauphiné Alps recommended him to Whymper, writing
that Croz was happy only "when upward of ten thousand

J.-A. Carrel (seated). (Courtesy of V. Sella, Biella)

feet high." In *Scrambles*, Whymper notes, "I know what my friend meant. Croz was happiest when employing his powers to the utmost. Places where you and I would 'toil and sweat and yet be freezing cold' were bagatelles to him, and it was only when he got above the range of ordinary mortals and was required to employ his magnificent strength and to draw upon his unsurpassed knowledge of ice and snow that he could be said to be really and truly happy. Of all the guides with whom I have traveled, Michel Croz was the man who was most after my own heart. He did not work like a blunt razor and take to his toil unkindly. He did not need urging or to be told a second time to do anything. You had but to say *what* was to be done and *how* it was to be done, and the work *was* done if it was possible. Such men are not common, and when they are known they are valued. Michel was not widely known, but those who did know him came again and again. The inscription placed upon his tomb truthfully records that he was 'beloved by his comrades and esteemed by travelers.' "

That summer and in the first part of the 1865 season, Whymper compiled an astonishing record of first ascents in the Alps, mostly with Croz. During an eighteen-day period of almost unbroken good weather in the early summer of 1865, he climbed a total of nearly a hundred thousand vertical feet. He drew up a list of all the major unclimbed mountains in the Chamonix region—the Aiguille Verte, the Grandes Jorasses, Mont Dolent, and so on—and climbed them one after another. And at this time, he made a crucial discovery about the Matterhorn. The Matterhorn is a very deceptive mountain when looked at from a distance. It appears to be a solid monolith, whereas in fact it is very unstable and subject to constant erosion, which manifests itself in almost continuous rock and ice falls. Moreover, all the early expeditions had concentrated on the Italian side, which, in profile, appeared to be the only one with any kind of accessibility; from the Swiss side the east face, which towers over Zermatt, looks absolutely smooth and overwhelming. Nevertheless, Whymper, who was a very intelligent man as well as a courageous one, had begun studying the east face carefully. "The east face had been dismissed out of hand primarily because of its apparent smoothness, but of late Whymper had noted that the rock strata dipped outwards on the Italian side of the mountain, which inspired the logical reflection that they must dip inwards on the Zermatt side," Smythe writes. "Furthermore, his observant eye had noted that large beds of snow cling permanently to the east face even during a hot, dry summer, which suggested that the angle of the face was unlikely to exceed 45°. Lastly, he had ascended the slopes above the Zmutt glacier, whence the east face is visible in profile, and had noted that in general angle it was much less steep than it appeared when viewed from Zermatt . . . indeed, not more than 40°." To climb four thousand feet at an angle of forty degrees was still a formidable feat, but inspection showed that outcropping rocks broke the climb into a large number of almost stairlike ledges, which looked extremely attractive for climbing. Nonetheless, the guides were dead set against the climb— Carrel because he wanted the mountain to be climbed first from Italy, and the others because of the traditional reputation of the east face.

In the second week in July, Whymper was in Zermatt ready for another go at the Matterhorn. Since Croz had a prior commitment in Chamonix, Whymper had arranged to go with Carrel. At just this time an Italian climber, Felice Giordano, had organized a well-equipped party with the express purpose of beating Whymper to the Matterhorn, but from the Italian side. He too wanted the services of Carrel, and, yielding to his sense of patriotism, Carrel decided to go with the Italians. Whymper first learned of this when he met Giordano's caravan, including the Carrels, as it was moving toward the base of the Italian side of the Matterhorn. On pressing Carrel, he was told that this engagement "with a family of distinction" had been of long standing but the date had been left open and the matter had only been settled the day before. Whymper, of course, felt betrayed. This, and his sense of frustration at the prospect of losing the Matterhorn, undoubtedly accounted for Whymper's subsequent willingness to join with several English climbers, some of whom were quite inexperienced, in an effort to outrace the Italians from the Swiss side. The first member of the future party appeared on the scene almost at once. He was Lord Francis Douglas, the eighteen-year-old brother of the Marquis of Queensberry. Douglas had started climbing two years earlier and had engaged the well-known

Zermatt guide, "Old" Peter Taugwalder ("Young" Peter, Taugwalder's son, also joined the group, first as a porter, then as a guide), for an attempt on the Swiss side of the Matterhorn, which Old Peter, after some preliminary exploration, had decided was climbable. Whymper and Douglas agreed to join forces. Soon after, Croz, himself, showed up (his original engagement in Chamonix having terminated more quickly than he had expected) with two clients, the Reverend Charles Hudson, one of the strongest contemporary English climbers, and his protégé D. R. Hadow, who was nineteen and had made only one previous climb, the Mont Blanc. They too were planning to climb the Matterhorn, but after some conferences, Whymper and Hudson agreed that it was foolish to have two independent parties operating on the same ridge at the same time, and they decided to do the climb together. However, Whymper had serious misgivings about Hadow's inexperience and about the size of the group.

On the morning of July 13th, this unwieldy group left Zermatt carrying nearly six hundred feet of climbing rope pieced off into sections. Much of the rope was new, but there was one very poor section, which they probably were not expecting to make much use of. The first day they moved easily to a flat place on the ridge, at eleven thousand feet, and decided to bivouac there for the night. Croz and Young Peter were sent ahead to scout the route, and when they returned they announced that the whole climb appeared quite feasible and that they might well have gone all the way to the summit that very day. The description in *Scrambles* of the ascent itself, which took place the next day, takes no more than a page or so, for the simple reason that the east face turned out to be even easier than Whymper had imagined. At 1:40 P.M. of July 14th, he and his companions stood at the top. Whymper's first thought was of Carrel. He writes:

It was not yet certain that we had not been beaten. The summit of the Matterhorn was formed of a rudely level ridge, about three hundred and fifty feet long, and the Italians might have been at its farther extremity. I hastened to its southern end, scanning the snow right and left eagerly. Hurrah again! It was untrodden! "Where were the men?" I peered over the cliff, half doubting, half expectant. I saw them immediately, mere dots on the ridge at an immense distance below. Up went my arms and my hat. "Croz! Croz! Come here!" "Where are they, Monsieur?" "There—don't you see them down there?" "Ah, the *coquins!* They are low down." "Croz, we must make those fellows hear us." We yelled until we were hoarse. The Italians seemed to regard us—we could not be certain. "Croz, we *must* make them hear us—they *shall* hear us!" I seized a block of rock and hurled it down and called upon my companions, in the name of friendship, to do the same. We drove our sticks in and prized away the crags, and soon a torrent of stones poured down the cliffs. There was no mistake about it this time. The Italians turned and fled. Still I would that the leader of that party could have stood with us at that moment, for our victorious shouts conveyed to him the disappointment of a lifetime. He was *the* man of all those who attempted the ascent of the Matterhorn who most deserved to be first upon its summit. He was the first to doubt its inaccessibility, and he was the only man who persisted in believing that its ascent would be accomplished.

After an hour on the summit, the party started down—Croz in the lead (a curious order, since on the descent the stronger climbers ordinarily go last), then Hadow, Hudson, and Douglas, with the two Taugwalders and Whymper bringing up the rear. Presently, they came to some tricky rock and started descending it with only one man moving at a time. What happened next can best be described by Whymper:

> A sharp-eyed lad ran into the Monte Rosa hotel [in Zermatt] . . . saying that he had seen an avalanche fall from the summit

of the Matterhorn onto the Matterhorn Glacier. The boy was reproved for telling idle stories; he was right, nevertheless, and this was what he saw: Michel Croz had laid aside his axe and, in order to give Mr. Hadow greater security, was absolutely taking hold of his legs and putting his feet, one by one, into their proper positions. As far as I know, no one was actually descending. I cannot speak with certainty, because the two leading men were partially hidden from my sight by an intervening mass of rock, but it is my belief from the movements of their shoulders that Croz, having done as I said, was in the act of turning round to go down a step or two himself; at this moment, Mr. Hadow slipped, fell against him, and knocked him over. I heard one startled exclamation from Croz, then saw him and Mr. Hadow flying downward. In another moment, Hudson was dragged from his steps, and Lord F. Douglas immediately after him. All this was the work of a moment. Immediately we heard Croz's exclamation, Old Peter and I planted ourselves as firmly as the rocks would permit; the rope was taut between us, and the jerk came on us both as on one man. We held, but the rope broke midway between [Young Peter] Taugwalder and Lord Francis Douglas. For a few seconds, we saw our unfortunate companions sliding downward on their backs and spreading out their hands, endeavoring to save themselves. They passed from our sight uninjured, disappeared one by one, and fell from precipice to precipice on to the Matterhorn Glacier below, a distance of nearly four thousand feet in height. From the moment the rope broke, it was impossible to help them. So perished our comrades!

Whymper writes that for half an hour the survivors remained paralyzed, "without moving a single step," while the two Taugwalders cried like infants. "Old Peter rent the air with exclamations of 'Chamounix!—Oh, what will Chamounix say?' He meant, 'Who would believe that Croz could fall?'" At last, they began to descend. Whymper saved a piece of the frayed rope, realizing that many questions about the fall would have to be answered. The descent was painfully slow. Part of that night was spent camped on the mountain. Indeed, they took the precaution of attaching fixed ropes wherever possible. Young Peter Taugwalder began to recover his nerve, and, according to Whymper soon conceived the notion that the fall would make him famous, and that he could earn money as a celebrity. This incensed Whymper. "They filled the cup of bitterness to overflowing," he writes, "and I tore down the cliff madly and recklessly, in a way that caused them more than once to inquire if I wished to kill them."

The next day, a search party, which included Whymper, found the broken bodies of all the men, except Douglas, and some of their personal effects buried in the snow at the base of the mountain. A brief ceremony was read from Hudson's prayer book, which was recovered on the glacier. And, sometime later, the bodies were returned to Zermatt for burial in the local cemetery. Whymper ends *Scrambles* with the words:

> Still the last sad memory hovers round and sometimes drifts across like floating mist, cutting off sunshine and chilling the remembrance of happier times. There have been joys too great to be described in words, and there have been griefs upon which I have not dared to dwell, and with these in mind I say, climb if you will, but remember that courage and strength are naught without prudence, and that a momentary negligence may destroy the happiness of a lifetime. Do nothing in haste, look well to each step, and from the beginning think what may be the end.

Whymper worked unflaggingly to raise money for Croz's sisters in Chamonix and did everything possible to safeguard Old Peter's reputation at the subsequent inquest: while Young Peter continued to guide in Zermatt, Old Peter left Switzerland to return only at the end of his life. Two days after the accident, ironically, Carrel succeeded in climbing, by an immensely difficult route, the Italian side of the Matterhorn.

The effect of Whymper's accident on English climbing can be judged by the account of W. A. B. Coolidge, whose climbing career began at about that time. In *The Alps in Nature and History,* he recalls:

The present writer . . . was one of the earliest recruits to mountaineering after *the* accident, and went on climbing for thirty-three years. Hence, he can recollect vividly the sort of palsy that fell upon the good cause after that frightful catastrophe of July 14, 1865, particularly amongst English climbers. Few in numbers, all knowing each other personally, shunning the public gaze as far as possible (and in those days it *was* possible to do so), they went about under a sort of dark shade, looked on with scarcely disguised contempt by the world of ordinary travellers. They, so to speak, climbed on sufferance, enjoying themselves much, it is true, but keeping all expressions of that joy to themselves in order not to excite derision. . . . Two personal experiences may illustrate this sorrowful period in the history of climbing. Early in July, 1868, the present writer met, in the Gleckstein cave on the Wetterhorn, Mr. Julius Elliott (who was killed next year on the Schreckhorn). In the course of conversation, Mr. Elliott revealed, almost under the seal of confession, his strong desire, even his fixed intention, to attempt shortly the Matterhorn from the Swiss side. This feat he achieved a fortnight later, this being the first complete ascent on that side since the accident. It caused a very great sensation, as it proved that the expedition was not so absolutely certain to end fatally as had been imagined by many. The charm had been broken, but it required a man of strong will to break it. Some years later, in 1871, when it fell the turn of the present writer to ascend the Matterhorn, it was still considered a most remarkable thing

69

that within the same week *two* ascents of the dreaded peak
should have been made with complete success.

Armand Charlet, who is generally regarded as the greatest of the prewar Chamonix guides, recalls in his autobiography, *Vocation Alpine*, the violent reactions that were
produced among the Chamonix guides with whom he grew
up whenever Whymper's name was mentioned. Charlet was
able to see "*the* accident" through the eyes of the elders in his
family, who were among the outstanding Chamonix guides
at the time of Whymper's climb. Charlet's great-uncle Gaspard Simond, who climbed Mont Blanc fifty-five times, retained to the end of his life an astonishing ability to
remember the events of his childhood and youth. (He had
an especially vivid recollection of a visit to Chamonix by
Napoleon III and Empress Eugénie in 1860; all the children
of the village were paraded before Their Majesties, and,
much to Gaspard's surprise, each child was handed a silver
coin. Knowing a good thing when he saw it, Gaspard
changed his clothes and presented himself for a second
coin, which he was duly awarded.) His great-nephew
writes:

> More than fifty years after, I still hear their passionate
> discussions; above all, those between my grandfather and
> Uncle Gaspard, who, like all the important Chamonix guides
> of the time, believed firmly in the culpability of Whymper
> and his guides. They used to cite the words of Taugwalder:
> "What are they going to say in Chamonix?" . . . Frédéric
> Payot, Charlet-Straton, and many others, whose names I have
> forgotten, were, like Uncle Gaspard, convinced of Whymper's
> guilt, as well as that of the Taugwalders. Gaspard would get
> carried away and smash his fist on the table and swear in a
> way that would make all guides—past, present, and future—
> tremble. [His brother-in-law] Ambroise Ravanel retained his

sang-froid, offering calm arguments against the tirades of Gaspard, who saw red each time the name of Whymper was mentioned to him. At the age of twelve, perhaps before, without having read Whymper's version, I knew the names of all the members of the caravan, the order in which they were descending, and their worth as climbers. Often, Gaspard saved for the last his most telling argument: "Croz ought to have been last on the rope. A man of his strength should not have been first on the descent; he could not have fallen." To which my grandfather would reply that he had not fallen, but that he had been pulled by surprise. Nothing would change him, and my uncle hung on to his opinion until the end of his life.

Whymper was, of course, deeply affected by the accident. He spent the rest of his life wandering around the world, a lonely figure, and though he continued to climb, he never again did so in Europe, except for a second ascent of the Matterhorn in 1874. The publication of his wonderfully illustrated *Scrambles* in 1871 was an immense success. It was translated into many languages, and helped break down the prejudice against climbing that had grown up since the Matterhorn accident. In 1879, Whymper and J.-A. and Louis Carrel (a cousin) made a long and successful expedition to the Ecuadorian Andes, and from it emerged Whymper's second book, *Travels Amongst the Great Andes of the Equator*. During that trip, they climbed Chimborazo (20,498 feet), the first mountain over twenty thousand feet to be conquered. (In 1890, Carrel died of exhaustion after guiding a party to safety in a violent blizzard on the Matterhorn.) Later, Whymper returned to the Alps and wrote guidebooks to Chamonix and Zermatt. He became a celebrated Victorian figure, and an account of him at fifty-seven notes of his features, "They give the sort of vague impression one would have if a giant were smothered in rose leaves." At sixty-six,

Whymper married a girl of twenty-one. The marriage, his only one, produced a daughter, Ethel, who, in turn, became a climber. On September 16, 1911, Whymper died in a hotel room in Chamonix, and he is buried in a modest grave, among many other climbers and guides, in a cemetery near the village.

A. F. Mummery's ascent of the Grépon on August 5, 1881, marks the beginning of the modern era of mountain climbing. Mummery himself was the epitome of the late-nineteenth-century British climber, for now the whole attitude toward climbing had changed. It had become a sport and a challenge. As Mummery wrote in the preface to his mountaineering classic, *My Climbs in the Alps and Caucasus*: "I fear no contributions to science or topography or learning of any sort are to be found sandwiched in between the story of crags and *séracs* [great blocks of ice], of driving storm and perfect weather. To tell the truth, I have only the vaguest ideas about theodolites, and as for plane tables their very name is an abomination. To those who think with me, who regard mountaineering as unmixed play, these pages are alone addressed." Moreover, a whole new style of mountain climbing had arisen from this change in attitude. As few people as possible were taken along on an expedition, and, except for the inevitable victory champagne, as few provisions. In the last chapter of his book, Mummery argues against the then widely accepted dictum that three people was the absolute minimum number of people for any expedition involving glacier climbing. He insists that a party of two is safer, one reason being that two people have more mobility if, for example, they are caught in an avalanche. "Every additional man on the rope means a serious decrease of the extreme speed at which the party can move," he says, "and it is in speed, and in speed alone, that a party so

surprised can hope for safety." In addition, the entire technique of climbing had been revolutionized between de
Saussure's day and Mummery's. In the beginning, guides
and climbers had literally hung on to one another while
climbing; the guides were equipped with long metal batons,
and the climbers clung to them for dear life. In the middle of
the nineteenth century, the climbing rope came into use,
meaning that climber and guide could be widely separated
during a climb. (De Saussure's guides did make some use of
short ropes, but only for hauling up climbers, who held on
to the free end.) Moreover, a rope permits so-called "artificial" climbing, in which the climber makes use of the rope
not only as a security measure (the modern rope is generally
made of nylon and has a breaking strength of about two
tons) but as a direct climbing aid. The oldest of the "artificial" techniques is the rappel, which came into wide use in
Chamonix in the eighteen-seventies. This is a means of
descending walls of rock or ice that are essentially vertical—
in fact, the more nearly vertical the better. The rope is fas-
tened at some point above the descent (on ice, one sometimes carves out an ice "mushroom" to use as an anchor, for,
ideally, the rope is run around some sort of object in a great
U-shaped loop, so that it can be recovered from the bottom
by pulling one end), and the climber runs the rope between
his legs and into a kind of loop around his shoulders. He can
then slide down it freely, using the friction of his hands as a
brake whenever he wants to stop. It is a spectacular but
entirely safe operation, and one that enables a climber to go
down otherwise impossible faces. As for the long baton of de
Saussure's guides, it has gradually evolved into the modern
ice axe—an instrument about three feet long, with a sharp
point at one end and two axelike blades at the other for
gripping the snow or cutting steps in ice. In Mummery's
day, the ice axe was not very different from the contempo-

rary version, except that it was a good deal longer and more cumbersome. As for shoes, de Saussure wore low-cut ones with cleated soles, plus a kind of puttee to keep out the snow. He had a primitive version of what is known as a "crampon," or, in the lingo of the modern French climber, "*un crabe.*" This is a kind of metal frame with sharp points that is strapped over an ordinary shoe. De Saussure's crampons had only four points; the modern crampon has ten— long and very sharp. It is made of lightweight steel and is easily adjustable by a system of straps and buckles. The British rock climbers of Mummery's day always took a pair of tennis shoes along for very acrobatic climbing, so there was a good deal of changing of shoes on the mountainsides. In that era, the soles of the climbing boot were hobnailed, representing a compromise between a crampon and something that would hold on rock. Just after the Second World War, the Italian mountaineer Vitale Bramani introduced a sole with heavy rubber cleats. These soles, now universally used, get a very good grip on rock; on ice and snow the climber resorts to crampons. Pre-Mummery climbers carried ladders and wooden wedges—the ladders used for crossing crevasses or climbing very difficult walls, and the wedges used for additional footing after being hammered into cracks. Today, the ladders have just about been abandoned (although small rope ladders are sometimes used in artificial climbing), and the wedges have been largely supplanted by the metal piton. Pitons are wedges themselves—long, thin metal ones with a detachable ring at one end—and come in all sizes; one variety can be screwed into ice. A rope can be run through the ring, thus providing security for difficult climbing. In addition, all the auxiliary equipment has become lighter and vastly more efficient. In his book, for instance, Mummery often refers to the annoyances of the folding lanterns he had to use to pick his way across glaciers at night; today, of course, he would have a powerful lightweight flashlight.

Mummery, who was born in 1855, discovered the Alps at the age of fifteen, and fell in love with them with a passion that, he says, only grew with the years. He had made a number of lesser climbs when, in 1879, he decided to try a new route on the Matterhorn—the Zmutt ridge, which had been rejected by Whymper as "inaccessible." Arriving in Zermatt, he looked around for a suitable guide with whom to undertake such an adventure. His book contains a wonderful description of his first encounter with Alexander Burgener of Saas Fee, a village adjacent to Zermatt, who subsequently joined Mummery to become a member of one of the greatest climbing teams in the history of alpinism. Burgener was already a famous guide, having made the first ascent of the Grand Dru, in Chamonix, the previous year. "The broad-shouldered Alexander, his face half hidden in beard, was then interviewed," Mummery writes, and continues:

> He bluntly expressed his opinion that to go on such an expedition with a *Herr* of whom he knew nothing would be a *verfluchte Dummheit* [a confounded stupidity]. I was much taken by this bold expression of opinion, which appeared to me not merely indicative of a wise distrust of an untried climber, but also of a determination to drive home the attack, when once begun, to the utmost limits of possibility. My previous experience had been chiefly, if not exclusively, with men who were eager to start on any attempt, no matter how desperate, and who were far too polite to inquire whether their employer knew anything about the art of climbing. At an early stage in the proceedings, however, these men had invariably developed a most touching, but nonetheless most inconvenient, affection for their wives and families, and were compelled by these most commendable feelings to discontinue the ascent. The confident carriage of Alexander, and the

honest outspokenness of his language, seemed to show that he was not of this sort, and to presage well for our future acquaintance. I gladly accepted his suggestions, and agreed that we should make a few preliminary expeditions together.

From the beginning, Burgener and Mummery hit it off, and after a few experimental climbs they tackled and conquered the Zmutt ridge. Soon after this, they added a third man to the team—Benedikt Ventez, who was a rock climber of brilliant natural ability. It frequently happened in their climbs that Ventez would lead the way up a very difficult bit with Burgener prodding him figuratively, and sometimes literally, with his ice axe. Both Burgener and Ventez were superstitiously religious men, and in one curious episode, when they saw a light (which later turned out to be a lantern) moving on the glacier below the Matterhorn, they insisted that it was a ghost and demanded to return to the valley. Mummery writes, "The position was serious enough in all conscience. It is a well-ascertained fact (attested by all the ecclesiastical authorities of the Saas, Zermatt, and Anzasca valleys) that anyone seeing a *Geist* is certain to be killed within twenty-four hours! I pointed out to Burgener that this being so, there could be no advantage in turning back, for, either they were ghosts, in which case we must be killed, or they were not ghosts, in which case we might as well go on." Mummery's logic carried the day, and they went on to finish the climb. There is still a deep religious feeling among the Swiss guides, who will almost never climb on Sunday and who observe all religious holidays scrupulously.

In the summer of 1880, the team of Mummery, Burgener, and Ventez began the series of climbs that ultimately led to the summit of the Grépon. The Grépon is connected by a narrow broken ridge to a group of neighboring peaks called the Grands Charmoz. In Mummery's time, the Grépon and the Charmoz were regarded as part of the same aiguille, the two being simply called Les Charmoz. However, they proved to have such different "personalities," as one French writer put it, that they are now distinguished. The Charmoz is a craggy mass with numerous spikelike summital points, while the Grépon is a monolithic granite block with almost perfectly smooth sides. Its top, though, also consists of rocklike towers not directly accessible from one to another. In 1880, nobody had the slightest idea which of the towers was highest, and when Mummery began his climbs of the Grépon it was not clear where the summit was. First, Mummery and his guides tackled the Charmoz. It was a tremendous climb. At one point, they encountered a smooth green bulge of ice overhanging an almost vertical gully, and Ventez went on ahead to struggle with it while Burgener seconded him from below. Mummery writes:

> Some ten minutes later, both men appeared to my inexperienced eye in extremely critical positions. Ventez, almost without hold of any sort, was gradually nearing the aforementioned green bulge; an axe, skillfully applied by Burgener to that portion of the guide costume most usually decorated by patches of brilliant and varied hue, supplied the motive power, whilst Burgener himself was cleverly poised on invisible notches cut in the thin ice which glazed the rock. Before, however, Ventez could surmount the green bulge, it became necessary to shift the axe to his feet, and for a moment he was left clinging like a cat to the slippery wrinkles of the huge icicle. How he succeeded in maintaining his position is a mystery known only to himself and the law of gravity.

After some equally desperate encounters, the three men found themselves on the north summit of the Charmoz. Observers in Chamonix fired a cannon salute, and the trio returned triumphantly to the village.

The next summer, they were back for a try at the more formidable Grépon. Two Chamonix guides—Pierre Charlet and Prosper Payot—had climbed to a rock platform part way up the wall and had marked it with the initials "C.P." in red paint, and it is known as the C.P. to this day. In July, 1881, the British climbers F. M. and G. W. Balfour and their guides had pushed beyond the C.P. to a rock formation that they thought was the summit, only to learn that the true summit, which had been hidden during the climb, was twenty-three feet above them, at the top of a rock tower some thirty feet away and totally inaccessible. They contemplated piling up enough rocks to elevate the spot on which they were standing to a point above the true summit, but in the end they returned to the valley defeated. That summer, too, Mummery and his guides had made a futile attempt from the other side, facing the Mer de Glace, and had given up. (The Mer de Glace climb of the Grépon is still regarded as one of the most difficult in Chamonix, and is done only by absolutely first-rate rock climbers.) Then, on August 3rd, they started off for the northwest side of the Grépon. While climbing a glacier that led to the base of the mountain, they noticed that they were being raced up the glacier by another party. When the two groups met, Mummery reports, Burgener "found them to be led by a well-known Oberland guide." He goes on:

> We kept together as far as the foot of the couloir running up to the Charmoz-Grépon col. Here our ways diverged, so with mutual goodbyes, and wishing each other all sorts of luck and success, we parted company, the Oberlander first giving Burgener much good advice and ending by strongly advising him to abandon the attempt, "for," said he, "I have tried it, and where I have failed no one else need hope to succeed." Burgener was greatly moved by this peroration, and I learnt from a torrent of unreportable patois that our fate was sealed,

and even if we spent the rest of our lives on the mountain (or in falling off it), it would, in his opinion, be preferable to returning amid the jeers and taunts of this unbeliever.

They climbed the Charmoz-Grépon col and were faced by a monolithic vertical rock wall that no one else had been able to deal with. At this point, Ventez made a crucial discovery—a thin crack, practically vertical, that led up to a platform from which the summit looked possible. This crack, now known as the Mummery Crack, proved to be the key to the mountain. It has become one of the most celebrated bits of climbing in the Alps. Henri Isselin, in a fascinating book called *Les Aiguilles de Chamonix*, says, "For certain people it is an interesting exercise, for others one of the most difficult tests," and quotes the climber Guido Rey, who was watching his guide at work in the Crack: "He elevated himself by jerks . . . stopped, regathered his forces, and gained anew a bit of height. His body twisted and turned. . . . At one time I saw him dive, at another time return to the surface like a swimmer. . . . One only heard the crunching of the nails on his shoes against the granite and the puffing of his breath." Isselin goes on to say, "George Ingle Fich, a future Himalayan, found no serious difficulty with it. He hardly needed three minutes to master the pass. On the other hand, G. W. Young [a famous English climber] watched a full hour while 'a line of valorous ladies . . . under the conduct of several Chamonix guides were able to reach the top.' " Finally, Isselin quotes an especially honest account by an anonymous climber:

> I was held at all sides—the rock under my feet, the rappel rope in my hands, the safety rope at my waist. All I had to do was climb. Evidently—it was as simple as *"bonjour."* But that combination of one's hands on the rope and one's foot against the rock is not the best. I went as fast as I could, but I

exhausted myself by overlooking most of the natural supports. There are a few—notably the rocks that have become
wedged in the crack and offer every security. The only trouble
is that there is room on them for only one foot. Now my arms
are literally cut off. I am a few feet from the guide, who is
encouraging me, but I would give everything I have to be
finished with it. I am out of breath and exhausted. I beg for a
couple of seconds of rest, and then I heave myself with a
desperate effort onto the platform above, in the state more of
a package than a hero, so exhausted that I can hardly untie
the rope and sit down.

With typical understatement, Mummery makes light of
his climb up the fissure, saying merely that soon the three
men were able to complete their climb to the north summit
of the Grépon. But was the north summit the true summit?
Upon his return to Chamonix later that day, the question
began to haunt Mummery, and he reports that he had a
troubled vision that night of a great square tower near the
one they had actually climbed. Was *this* the real summit?
Nothing would do but to make another attempt the next day.
On the previous climb, Burgener had severely damaged the
seat of his pants, so a day's delay was necessary while a tailor
made repairs. The following day, the three repeated the
climb and found themselves at the base of the tower that had
haunted Mummery's sleep. He reports, "It was certainly one
of the most forbidding rocks I have ever set eyes on. Unlike
the rest of the peak, it was smooth to the touch, and its
square-cut edges offered no hold or grip of any sort." For a
while, they tried to throw a rope over the tower, so that they
could haul themselves up by it, but they had no success, so
Ventez was sent on ahead. For the first few feet, Burgener
was able to help him with the axe, but when Ventez got
beyond Burgener's reach he had to call on his extraordinary
natural skills to negotiate the rest of the passage, while his

two colleagues watched anxiously. Finally, he made it and lowered the rope to the two others. When the three of them reached the top, they found it to be of "palatial dimensions and . . . provided with three stone chairs." Mummery adds, "The loftiest of these was at once appropriated by Burgener for the ice axe, and the inferior members of the party were bidden to bring stones to build it securely in position. This solemn rite being duly performed, we stretched ourselves full length and mocked M. Couttet's popgun at Chamonix with a pop of far more exhilarating sort."

Upon his return to Chamonix, Mummery announced that he would pay a thousand francs—a sizable sum then— to the man who could recover the axe. This, oddly enough, turned out to be Charlet's Uncle Gaspard. In 1885, Henri Dunod, a young French officer in the Chasseurs Alpins, decided to take up Mummery's challenge, and he hired François and Gaspard Simond to accompany him. Dunod had with him a flag that he intended to leave at the summit in place of the axe, and the two guides took along a veritable storehouse of ladders and other equipment, because they had heard, erroneously, that Mummery had used ladders in making the climb. They never imagined that the Mummery Crack was the route to the summit, simply overlooking it as they tried to find a way up the face. They found none, and on August 11th they were back for another attack. This time, luck was with them, for an enormous boulder had fallen and provided a natural bridge between the C.P. and the face. They managed to get to the summit ridge, but bad weather overtook them before they could make an attempt on the tower, from whose summit the silhouette of Mummery's axe taunted them. Finally, on September 2nd, they made a fourth attempt, and Dunod, weeping with emotion, was able to replace Mummery's ice axe with the flag. Upon returning to the valley, Gaspard set out to present Mummery with the axe, only to be informed that the offer had held good for just one season, and that since four years had passed, it was no longer valid. Gaspard's emotions can be imagined, and his great-nephew reports that for years afterward he would explode with "*Ce bougre de Mummery!*" every time Mummery's name was mentioned. Even so, Gaspard, who had seen Mummery in action as a climber, retained an immense admiration of his perfect mastery of both rock and ice.

From a present-day perspective, how difficult a climb was the Grépon? Actually, the question can be given a quite objective answer. Since 1933, all the climbs in Chamonix and all the different routes and sub-routes have been classified according to difficulty. The classes run from I to VI—easy, not hard, rather hard, hard, very hard, and extremely hard. Of course, there is a certain subjectivity in making such a classification, but there has been so much climbing on the Aiguilles de Chamonix by now that reasonably objective standards can be set. The climbs are all described with great thoroughness in a four-volume climbing guide called the *Guide Vallot* (named for the Vallot brothers, who made one of the first systematic surveys of the area, at the end of the nineteenth century). In it one finds almost microscopically detailed maps of the most difficult parts of a climb, and instructions like "Climb a vertical crack of twenty meters (Class III and IV) to a niche dominated by a vertical wall, then follow to left along a narrow terrace (Class IV, with three pitons) to an overhanging ridge." In addition, each climb is given an over-all grade, and there is an estimate of how long it should take. Ice climbs are given only general descriptions, because ice conditions change from day to day. Most of the present-day Chamonix guides and other climbers make careful annotations in their *Vallots* on climbs that are in any way novel, so that the edition can be kept up

to date. It is an immensely useful system, and it prevents—
or should prevent—climbers from tackling ascents that are
too difficult for them. The first edition of the *Guide* appeared
in 1925, and a little later Lucien Devies, who was president
of the French Alpine Club, made a kind of historical rating of
the pioneering climbs in the region. He found that the first
climb of the Aiguille du Midi by Malczewski was only a
Class I climb, and that all the climbs in the Victorian Age
until Mummery's were Class III at most. With Mummery,
the era of Class IV climbing began, the Grépon by way of the
Mummery Crack being a Class IV climb. The Grépon via the
Mer de Glace, which was first done in 1911, is a Class V
climb, one passage being so difficult that on the initial ascent
the lead man could get up it only by inserting the point of
his ice axe in a tiny fissure and using its handle for leverage.
On this face of the Grépon, there is a small climbing refuge,
La Tour Rouge, which has some Class IV passages leading
up to it. There are several Class VI climbs in the Chamonix
region. For example, in the "Ecclesiastical" Aiguilles, *Vallot*
lists L'Enfant de Chœur (first climbed in 1948 by the great
Chamonix guide Lionel Terray) as having a summit
passage—consisting of a smooth, vertical block covered
with black lichen—that is a pure VI.

With the end of the nineteenth century, the great era of
guided climbing approached its close. In the eighteen-
sixties and seventies, guides were regarded more or less as
family servants. They were sometimes hired for a whole
season but more usually for several weeks. Although the
guides and their clients often felt a good deal of respect for
each other, there was always—especially with the British
climbers—a social barrier that was not crossed. (Charlet's
grandfather was a well-educated man, and his erudition
used to come as something of a surprise to his clients. One

The Grépon as seen from the Mer de Glace. (Courtesy of Bradford Washburn)

day while he was conducting a party from a noble family on a mule trip, he pointed out to one of the women that she was holding her reins badly. By chance, he used the imperfect subjunctive in his admonition, and the woman was so surprised that she called to her husband, "We have a guide who employs the imperfect subjunctive!") Mummery was the first climber to do without guides on difficult climbs, and in the latter part of his career he came to despise them, for he felt that they had become simply climbing machines and were taking the sport away. In *My Climbs in the Alps and Caucasus*, he writes:

> The guide of the *Peaks, Passes,* and *Glaciers* age was a friend and adviser; he led the party and entered fully into all the fun and jollity of the expedition; on the return to the little mountain inn, he was still, more or less, one of the party, and the evening pipe could only be enjoyed in his company. Happy

amongst his own mountains and skilled in ferreting out all the slender resources of the village, he was an invaluable and most pleasant companion. But the advantage was not wholly on one side. Thrown constantly in contact with his employers, he acquired from them those minor rules of conduct and politeness which are essential if guide and traveller are to develop mutual friendship and respect. Of these early pioneers, Melchior Anderegg and a few others still remain; but amongst the younger men, there are none with whom one could associate on the old terms and with the old intimacy. The swarming of the tourist has brought with it the wretched distinctions of class, and the modern guide inhabits the guide's room and sees his Monsieur only when actually on an expedition. Cut off from the intercourse of the old days, the guide tends more and more to belong to the lackey tribe, and the ambitious tourist looks upon him much as his less aspiring brother regards the mule.

Mummery wrote *My Climbs in the Alps and Caucasus* in 1894, just before he embarked on a long-awaited expedition to the Himalayas. Characteristically, he had chosen to start out on one of the most difficult of all the Himalayan peaks— Nanga Parbat, which was not climbed until 1953. His letters home to his wife, published in the preface to the book, are full of the gaiety and casual understatement that were typical of him. In the last of them, probably written on August 23rd, he says, "I have had some slap-up climbs, and seen cliffs and *séracs* such as the Alps and Caucasus cannot touch." The next day, he disappeared with two Gurkhas into the whirling snows of Nanga Parbat, and they were never seen again. For all his optimism, Mummery seems to have had an odd foreboding of his death. He ends his book with a credo:

High proficiency in the sport is only attainable when a natural aptitude is combined with long years of practice, and not without some, perhaps much, danger to life and limb.

Happily, the faithful climber usually acquires this skill at an age when the responsibilities of life have not yet laid firm hold upon him, and when he may fairly claim some latitude in matters of this sort. On the other hand, he gains a knowledge of himself, a love of all that is most beautiful in nature, and an outlet such as no other sport affords for the stirring energies of youth; gains for which no price is, perhaps, too high. It is true the great ridges sometimes demand their sacrifice, but the mountaineer would hardly forgo his worship though he knew himself to be the destined victim.

PART TWO

Practice

3

Moi, Je Suis Optimiste

There is a Japanese proverb that says, "The man who has never climbed Fujiyama is a fool; the man who has climbed Fujiyama twice is twice a fool." I have never climbed Fujiyama, but I am sure that if I ever did, it would be once and with a guide. Most of my climbing experience has been on guided climbs. These began in 1937, when, at the age of seven, I was taken to climb the Visi Alp by a group of Englishpeople who were vacationing in the tiny Swiss mountaineering town of Kandersteg, in the Bernese Oberland. My parents were both sick and in the hospital near Bern, and my brother and I had been left in the care of a Swiss nurse in the Kurhaus in Kandersteg, where the English climbers were also staying. Our plight touched them, and since I was the elder, I was taken climbing. We ascended a small peak which they called the Visi Alp and I was given a solemn document, signed by forty members of the party, to prove that I had made the climb. I recently went back to Kandersteg and could not find the Visi Alp. (There is a Fisi Alp near Kandersteg and it may be in my certificate Fisi was turned into Visi.) Perhaps they made up the name for me. In any case, I climbed something. It was my initiation into the climbing of mountains, and it was a great experience.

Over the years, I have done a fair amount of climbing, but until 1963, when I began to learn the art from the guides at Chamonix, it was a hit-or-miss business, governed by the fact that guided climbing in the United States is confined to the West, whereas I live in the East. There are guides in the Rockies, in the Tetons of Wyoming, and in Mount Rainier National Park, in Washington. In Mount Rainier Park, the mountaineering conditions are similar to those in the Alps. Mount Rainier is glacierized and, as a climb, is quite similar in character to Mont Blanc, but the system of guides is very different. No group of climbers is permitted on Mount Rainier without first being approved by the Park Rangers, many of whom are guides. The Rangers check the equipment and experience of the party and decide whether they are adequate for the climb proposed. There is a stiff fine for climbing without permission. All this is done so that people who do not belong on the mountain do not get on it, and so that the Rangers won't have to risk their lives rescuing people who should not have been climbing in the first place. No such control exists in the Alps. Anyone can walk into any alpine station, with or without decent equipment, and climb anything. Many accidents occur—in a typical season there are some fifty fatal ones in Chamonix alone—and it is not difficult to understand why; rather, it is surprising that there aren't more. Frequently, climbers don't make up their minds where they are going until they get to the base of the mountains, and each year, as a result, a certain number of climbers simply disappear until their absence is noted by family or friends. I once asked one of the Chamonix guides—who at that time were largely responsible for rescue work— whether there had ever been an attempt to impose the Mount Rainier kind of restrictions on the climbers, and he pointed out that the sheer number of climbers would make this almost impossible; it would take an army to police them. During the climbing season—July and August— there are between three and four thousand climbers operating out of the Chamonix Valley every day.

There is also a less prosaic objection to any regimentation of climbing. Many guides and almost all climbers feel that mountaineering's greatest charm in this age of forms, documents, and restrictions is its freedom, and that to hem it in with inspections and permissions would be to destroy its meaning. In fact, mountaineering is now one of the most democratic of all sports. The era is past in which it was done only by a few wealthy eccentrics, like de Saussure, or by the English gentry, as in the middle of the last century. Now mountaineering in Europe is done by people from every imaginable walk of life. One may find a group of Scottish office workers like those I once met in a mountain hut above Chamonix. They had saved every extra penny for nearly a year in order to do six weeks of climbing, and they had calculated things so closely that they could not afford to take the train from Chamonix to the point where the trail up to their hut began. About once a week, they would descend on foot into the valley, buy all the food they needed for the coming week, and walk back up, carrying it on their backs— a stiff six- or eight-hour walk, all uphill. At the other extreme, one can still find perfectly equipped Continental climbers of the old school, with a guide for each member of the party and perhaps a porter or two (usually *aspirants*, or young guides in training) to carry auxiliary equipment like movie cameras. Indeed, the democracy of alpine climbing is movingly revealed in the accident reports that the European papers carry in the summer. All the Geneva papers have climbing sections, filled with alpine news. Some of the news consists of reporting first ascents by new routes. (In the summer of 1964, for example, the famous Italian guide Walter Bonatti and a well-known Genevan guide, Michel Vaucher, put up a remarkable new route on the north face of the Grandes Jorasses, near Chamonix. Because of bad weather, nothing was seen or heard of them for a few days, and for a while they were thought to have been killed in an avalanche. When they finally reappeared, it turned out that they had indeed been caught in an avalanche—one in which a rock the size of a small cathedral had fallen close to them and a shower of smaller rocks had cut their climbing rope—and had escaped only by a miracle. Vaucher said that the route was so dangerous he hoped no one else would ever try it.) Most of the news, however, consists of accident reports, and from them one can get a good idea of the variety of people who climb—a hairdresser from Lausanne, a student from Munich, an Italian doctor and his son, and so on.

Climbing is the most beautiful sport I know, and also the most dangerous. If one loves the mountains and acknowledges the danger, one must make some sort of decision about whether and how to climb. My own decision is never to climb anything that poses technical difficulties without a professional guide, or at least without an amateur climber who is equal to a guide in experience. Until my arrival in Chamonix, this sage self-advice had confined me to sporadic climbing in the West, a meager ascent or two in the Alps with avuncular Swiss guides, and a climb of Memorial

Hall at Harvard with a roommate who was an expert mountaineer and a veteran of expeditions to the Himalayas and
Alaska. Climbing buildings is an old tradition at the major
British universities, and there are even printed guides detail-
ing the better climbs. A delightful description of the pleasures of building climbing at Cambridge University is
contained in *The Night Climbers of Cambridge*, by someone
who calls himself Whipplesnaith. Whipplesnaith's book—
illustrated with diagrammatic photographs bearing cap-
tions like "Third Court, St. John's: A difficult and exposed
climb; when the second climber was at B, six dons passed
underneath"—describes many of the better routes up the
various university landmarks, but he observes that not all
the true mountaineers at Cambridge were attracted to building climbing; the president of the Cambridge University
Mountaineering Club, for one, refused to take part in an
especially difficult ascent because, as he said, "I am not a cat
burglar." Building climbing was also a tradition at Harvard
until the university announced that anyone caught at it was
subject to instant expulsion. My roommate had had his
heart set on climbing Memorial Hall for several years, and he
proposed that we do it jointly just after we had taken our
final Ph.D. examinations (he is, like me, a physicist) and just
before we were formally awarded our degrees. His logic was
that if we were caught, it was quite unlikely that the university would throw us out only a few days before we were
admitted into the community of scholars. With some misgivings, I accepted this reasoning, and on a moonless night
in late May of 1955, equipped with a strong climbing rope,
we set off. The climb, which was done with the aid of several
fixed ladders and scaffolds, was much easier than I had
expected, and we found ourselves somewhere under the
clock in the tower at about two in the morning. After contemplating the peaceful Cambridge scene and listening to

two strokes of the clock, we returned to street level, unharmed and undetected.

This was where things stood until 1963, when I began climbing in Chamonix. I first went to Chamonix in 1959, when I was working at CERN, the nuclear laboratory in Geneva. Like most of the other people at the laboratory, I used to spend the weekends walking around in the neighboring mountains, and one weekend early in the summer I drove to Chamonix, through the lovely farming country of the French Savoie. For most of the drive, one does not see the high mountains, because they are blocked by the nearby hills. Then, suddenly, the country opens up, and Mont Blanc and some of the neighboring aiguilles stand out silhouetted fantastically against the sky. Ever since the early eighteenth century, visitors to the valley have traveled this route, come to this same place, and felt the same sense of wonder. The mountains are again lost sight of as one enters the Chamonix Valley and drives up the winding road toward the town, but soon they reappear, even more splendid than before. Chamonix itself comes as something of a disappointment. It is now frankly a tourist town, with innumerable hotels, little souvenir shops, movie houses, and the like. When one gets to know it better, though, one can begin to distinguish the parts that represent the underlying mountain life from the parts that are there just to catch the tourist's eye.

As with many tourists, my first experience with the mountains was a trip on the *téléphérique* that leads from the valley to the top of the Aiguille du Midi, which hovers over the town. From the top, I took one of the small *télécabines*, suspended from a cable, over the glaciers to the Italian frontier. (During the summer of 1962 the cable was cut by a low-flying French Air Force jet, and several people were killed. A Chamonix guide who happened to be riding in one of the cable cars climbed hand over hand down the broken cable onto the glacier to get help.) Having looked at the rugged and forbidding quality of the terrain from these various *téléphériques*, I decided that Chamonix climbing was too much for me, and that I would content myself with exploring as much of the country as possible on simple walks. But by the summer of 1963 I had exhausted all the trails, and it was a question of either learning to climb in the valley or going somewhere else.

Early that summer, therefore, I dropped in at the Bureau des Guides in Chamonix. At this time, the Bureau was situated near the church in the center of town. (It has now moved into more elegant quarters at one end of the fashionable Hôtel du Mont-Blanc, even nearer the church.) There was no one inside, but soon a trim, dark, shortish man emerged from the café across the street. (I later found out that this was known among the guides as the "annex"; now the annex has also moved—to the elegant bar of the hotel.) He identified himself as Nicolau Barthélémy, Chef des Guides, and asked if he could be of assistance. I told him that I wanted to start at the beginning and learn enough about climbing to be able to do a few modest climbs in the region. He said that this sounded like a very sensible idea to him, and that if I would return to the Bureau at two-thirty that afternoon he would have a guide there to begin *l'école d'escalade*. The cost, he told me, would be twenty-four francs an hour—something less than five dollars. This is a relatively expensive kind of guided climbing, since many climbs that last a day or more cost only eighty or a hundred francs. A climb of Mont Blanc—a trip that is spread over two days—then cost two hundred and seventy-four francs. Some climbs are so difficult that they are not listed in the price schedule and are subject to negotiation between client and guide.

At two-thirty, I showed up at the Bureau just in time to see a jaunty, slight, extremely cheerful-looking fellow in his late twenties drive up at breakneck speed in a battered Simca. (Although I would trust Chamonix guides anywhere in the mountains, a good deal of experience has convinced me that they do not have an entirely rational attitude toward automobiles.) Barthélémy introduced him to me as my guide, Henri Dufour, and I got into the car. While we were careering through Chamonix, Dufour explained to me that *"l'école d'escalade"* referred to a nearby set of cliffs, about three hundred feet high, which were more properly known as Les Gaillands. Their present function was conceived some forty years ago by a Chamonix guide named Alfred Couttet, who put up the standard routes on their face and began using them systematically as a training area. Today, the cliff faces are covered with iron rings that have been cemented into place to provide an infallible means of belaying neophytes who have a tendency to fall off. There are all sorts of routes on the cliffs, ranging in difficulty from Class II and III (known as *moyenne montagne*) to Class V and V-Supérieur— just below Class VI, which is the hardest climb possible without the direct aid of special equipment such as rope ladders—"artificial" climbing. There are artificial routes on Les Gaillands that are classified separately—A-1, A-2, and so on. A climber who is expert in artificial techniques can go up practically any face, no matter how steep, provided that it has fissures into which he can drive his pitons. Dufour picked a Class II-III route, tied a rope around me, and shot up the face like a cat. In all guided climbing, the guide generally advances as far as the rope that connects him to his client will allow—a distance that French climbers call *"une longueur"*—and then waits until the client has climbed to where he is. Except on easy terrain, there is never more than one person in motion at a time. The first man has the responsibility of seeing to it that the second man is secured in case of a fall. When Dufour had anchored himself in, he called down to me to follow, instructing me to keep my body as far away from the rock as possible and to use my hands as little as possible. The beginner has a tendency to clutch at the rock with his hands and knees. This is bad, because one's knees supply very little traction, one is off balance, and it is impossible to see what one is doing. Using the hands is very tiring, and, besides, there is very little to hold on to anyway on any passage that is Class IV or over. The trick is to keep one's center of gravity over one's shoes, so that they are pressed firmly against the granite; a good rock climber appears to move like a man going up a ladder, using the wall as if it had rungs. On this occasion, I followed Dufour's instructions as best I could, and was soon beside him. He then started up the next *longueur,* and I was left to contemplate the scenery. I felt an increasing detachment from the earth, but this was diminished when I noticed a group of schoolchildren down below who had stopped to watch us. They were gathered in a ring—perhaps praying. (Watching climbers on Les Gaillands is one of the most popular spectator sports in Chamonix, and on a pleasant Sunday afternoon there may be a thousand people gathered below.)

Dufour had now reached another anchoring point and gave me a call to follow, but, try as I might, I was absolutely unable to see how to do so. Everywhere I looked there was nothing but smooth rock. Dufour called down, *"Regardez vos pieds!,"* and looking in the general direction of my feet I saw a minuscule outcropping of granite nearby that might provide room for part of one foot. I moved onto it, and then from it I suddenly saw a series of footholds and tiny handholds leading up to Dufour's perch. I have recalled de Saussure's phrase "the alternation of hope and fear" many times, and as I moved up to where Dufour was, it flashed through my mind once again. The rest of the climb was easy, and afterward Dufour said that he thought I was ready to try one of the simpler aiguilles. He gave me a list to choose from, and I selected the Aiguille de l'M, so called because of its M-shaped twin peaks. Though it is one of the smaller Chamonix aiguilles, it dominates the valley, and I had often studied it on my wanderings. We agreed to meet at the Aiguille du Midi *téléphérique* at seven the next morning— early enough to start on a short climb like this, because the *téléphérique* would take us to a point just an hour's walk from the base of the climb.

When Dufour appeared at the *téléphérique* station, he was warmly greeted by a vast horde of climbers, and was asked dozens of questions about the conditions of various routes in the massif, which he answered amiably. (In general, the guides are very willing to supply information to any climber.) At the top, we walked rapidly to the glacier leading to the base of the Aiguille de l'M. Dufour, who is a crack skier and (like nearly half the Chamonix guides) earns his living in the winter as a ski instructor, skied on the soles of his boots down a short but steep path leading to the glacier, while I followed more sedately. We crossed the glacier and climbed up to a relatively narrow ridge that on one side drops about twenty-five hundred feet straight down. Dufour pointed out some of the splendors of the view, while I stared apprehensively at the vertical face we were about to ascend. There were climbers everywhere on the ridge, mostly eating and drinking and adjusting their equipment. It is a starting point for all sorts of climbs, and is where one leaves all but the equipment one needs for the actual climb. I had been told that it is the responsibility of the client to feed the guide, and had brought along enough food for breakfast for the two of us, which we ate with our feet dangling into space.

After half an hour or so, Dufour announced that it was time to go to work. Most of the climb up the M consisted of passages whose difficulty was comparable to what we had done in practice, although I was very conscious, of course, that the distance down was perhaps ten times what it had been at Les Gaillands. At one point, we reached a kind of cave in the face, and Dufour, after planting me inside it, disappeared over the roof, leaving only the trail of rope as a clue to where he had gone. I called up to him asking for directions on how to proceed, and with (as I have come to recognize) typical guide humor, he called down from some-where that I was to *"suivez la corde"* ("Follow the rope"). Fortunately, two other climbers appeared at the entrance of the cave just then, and gave me somewhat more explicit advice on what to do. Soon I had joined Dufour, and we proceeded to the summit. The tops of the aiguilles are often very small, with room for only a couple of climbers at a time. We gave ourselves five minutes to admire the dizzying view of Chamonix below and then yielded our place to the next *"cordée."* On the way down, we took *"la voie normale,"* which, as Dufour remarked, is nearly a walk—*"presque touristique"*—and were soon back where we had left our gear.

On a neighboring aiguille, a tall guide with a great shock of blond hair was sitting on the top of a narrow pinnacle smoking a pipe and casually letting two clients down a vertical crack as if they were fish on a line. Dufour shouted *"Ay-o, Jaccoux!"* at him, and the two guides exchanged pleas-antries while the clients groped their way down the fissure. Dufour asked me if I would like to try that aiguille as well, but I felt that I had had enough for one day. (The idea of fumbling my way down the fissure in full view of nearly thirty climbers then assembled on the ridge did not espe-cially appeal to me, either.) On the way back to the *téléphé-*

rique station, Dufour stopped and pointed up to the face of the Aiguille du Midi. I barely made out four dots against the snow a few thousand feet above us. The dots—climbers doing the difficult ascent of the face—appeared to be stuck. We watched for ten minutes, during which they remained motionless, appearing to be almost nailed into the snow, and Dufour kept saying, "Not a great performance." I asked him if they would be able to move on, and he said simply, *"Il le faut."* As no news of them appeared later in the accident reports of the Geneva press, I assume they got up. Dufour and I returned to Chamonix by two o'clock, in time for a late lunch, and made a date to meet the next weekend. During the rest of the season, which was especially bad from the point of view of weather (in August it rained or snowed almost every day), I did a few more climbs of comparable difficulty, and that fall I returned to the United States a convert to at least the more rudimentary forms of Chamonix climbing.

Early in the summer of 1964, after putting in a week of hard walking to get into condition, I presented myself at the Bureau des Guides and asked Nicolau Barthélémy whether Dufour was available. He told me that Dufour had had a skiing accident during the winter and probably would not be able to work again until late in the summer, but that he would find me another guide. Out of curiosity, I asked him how climber and guide were matched, and he explained that the most common method was the *tour de rôle*, an institution that had begun almost with the founding of the Syndicat des Guides de Chamonix, in 1823. In essence, the *tour de rôle* is an evening roll call that begins where it left off the previous night. All the active guides in the Syndicat—now numbering about eighty, out of a total of a hundred and fifty nominal members—gather in the back room of the Bureau.

Barthélémy has a list of clients' requests for certain climbs, each written out on a white form. He reads the list of climbs from the forms and then begins the roll call. The first guide called has his pick of the climbs, the next his pick of what is left, and so on. As a rule, the older guides take the easier climbs. (Guides over sixty—and there are several very good ones—are required to have an annual physical examination.) The roll call, which Barthélémy let me observe a few times, is very amusing to watch, since there is a good deal of kidding about various guides' choice of climbs and a good deal of speculation about the quality of the climbers they are going to work for. (An amateur climber who acquires a poor reputation among the guides will soon find no one willing to go out with him.) In the old days, it was mandatory for every climb to be selected by the *tour de rôle*, but so many objections were raised by climbers who, having got used to a guide, wanted to retain him indefinitely that the regulation was abandoned, allowing one to hire a guide directly if one wants to.

As it was mid-June, there was still too much snow for any of the higher projects, and I had put in for the Clocher-Clochetons of Plan Praz, a short but technically difficult series of rock climbs in the Aiguilles Rouges. I had never seen them, but Barthélémy had suggested them as an excellent way to start the season. When I showed up the next morning, at seven, I was surprised to find that the guide I had drawn was none other than Claude Jaccoux, whom I had seen in action the previous year. We took a *télécabine* to Plan Praz and then walked for perhaps an hour to the base of the Clocher. The Clocher and the adjacent Clochetons are very sharply pointed miniature aiguilles that have the alarming look of giant rock fingers clawing their way out of the earth. Over the winter, I had forgotten how steep the faces of the aiguilles were, and I felt a sinking feeling on

101

The summit of the Aiguille du Plan. (Courtesy of Bradford Washburn)

looking at the vertical spire in front of us. Just then, I noticed a party of three moving slowly up the trail toward us. They seemed to be having some difficulty crossing the relatively easy terrain, and when they came alongside, the reason became clear. The middle man, strung between two guides, was blind. Jaccoux and I decided to give them the first crack at the face, and while the guides were getting their climbing ropes ready, I talked to their remarkable client. He told me that he had been an alpinist for many years before he lost his sight (he was Dutch and in his sixties), and that he still found pleasure in climbing. "Not seeing is an advantage for me," he said, "because I never know whether I am up or down, and therefore I'm never scared." One of the guides went on ahead to secure him, and the other one stayed just below him and adjusted his feet whenever he seemed to be

Claude Jaccoux at work.
(Courtesy of Claude
Jaccoux)

having difficulty finding a foothold. It was an all but incredible performance, and when they had got to the top, I felt that I could hardly do less. So, with Jaccoux shouting instructions and encouragement, I made the climb. Then there was the return trip to think about. The descent from the Clocher features an especially spectacular rappel. The Clocher rappel begins from a rock overhang, so that you get the impression of having to hurl yourself off into thin air, and when Jaccoux announced that I was to throw myself over the side, I thought at first that he was indulging in some kind of joke. But he pointed out that the route we had come up was obviously too difficult to go down (it is often possible, especially on rock, to go up faces that one cannot climb down), and that it was a matter of doing the rappel or waiting to be rescued. So I jumped, and after the first leap, to my surprise, I found bounding down the rock face on the rope quite pleasant.

On the way back to the *téléphérique*, I asked Jaccoux how he had become a guide. He said that he had been born in Sallanches, near Chamonix, but had moved to Paris when he was very young and thus—unlike most of the Chamonix guides, who learn to climb almost as soon as they are old enough to walk—had never climbed until he was eighteen. (He was then thirty-one.) At that time, he was studying literature at the Sorbonne, and a friend invited him to come climbing near Fontainebleau. There are a number of rock formations near Fontainebleau that have served as a training ground for hundreds of French climbers; in fact, it was a school of brilliant Fontainebleau rock climbers, led by the Parisian Pierre Allain and known as *"bleausards,"* who introduced artificial climbing to Chamonix. After a few trials, Jaccoux got to like climbing and has been at it ever since. On leaving the Sorbonne, he taught literature in a *lycée*, but he couldn't stand the monotony and has been a professional guide since 1961.

I asked Jaccoux how one advances from enthusiastic amateur climber to professional guide, and he said that it was a long process. Until the nineteen-forties, each guide bureau in France set its own standards, and candidates were trained informally, either by members of their family or by older guides. They then worked as porters until they had enough experience to be admitted as full-fledged guides. In 1943, the Vichy government drew up a law (still in force) that required all French guides to have a professional license, and a state school was created to train them. Because the Germans had closed the Mont Blanc massif to the French for strategic reasons, the school opened in La Grave, near Grenoble, in the Dauphiné Alps. After the war, it moved to

Chamonix and was amalgamated with a similar school to become the École Nationale de Ski et d'Alpinisme. To become a guide in France now, a man must first register at the school as an *aspirant*. He must be a citizen of France between the ages of eighteen and thirty-two, must have a medical certificate showing him to be physically capable of practicing mountaineering, and must have a certificate signed by three outstanding mountaineers attesting to his qualifications to become a guide. He must also submit a list of the climbs he has done. Then there is a stiff entrance examination. Those who pass it attend an intensive six-week course in which they learn not only climbing techniques but geology, meteorology, and mountain medicine—that is, first aid with special emphasis on frostbite, shock, and fractures. (All the guides carry an elaborate lightweight medical kit containing items like syringes of morphine and Coramine, used to combat the effects of shock and extreme fatigue.) There are also theoretical courses in the history of mountaineering. If a candidate passes all the examinations, he becomes an accredited *aspirant*. He is then allowed to act as a porter or a second to licensed guides, and to conduct some very simple climbs, such as training at Les Gaillands, but under no circumstance may he conduct any real guided climbs on his own. After no fewer than two and no more than five seasons as an *aspirant*, he is allowed to attempt to qualify for a guide rating. He returns to the E.N.S.A. for a one-month course, after which he is given a rigorous series of final examinations. It is not enough for someone to be simply an outstanding alpinist; what is much more important is that he want to practice the *métier* of guide—to conduct parties on all sorts of climbs, and not only the most difficult or technically interesting. In addition to all this, anyone who wants to become a Chamonix guide—that is, to be admitted to membership in the Syndicat—must be a native of the valley or the husband of a Chamonix girl; otherwise, he can be taken in only by the unanimous vote of the entire Syndicat at an assembly that is held every fall. In Jaccoux's case, Sallanches—twenty-two kilometers from Chamonix—was a bit beyond the outer limit of acceptable birthplaces for a man who wants to be a Chamonix guide without special pleading, but he was admitted to the Syndicat anyway. He served in the French Army for two and a half years, the first year in North Africa, where he managed to take time off to do some first ascents in the Atlas Mountains. During the rest of his Army career, he taught climbing at the École Militaire de Haute Montagne, also in Chamonix, which trains mountain troops. In effect, he practiced guiding while in the Army, and found that he liked it. One of his duties in the Army was to demonstrate high-altitude survival techniques to a group of British officers. Guides learn to construct igloos in case they are caught by a storm on a glacier—a very valuable skill that has saved many lives. In this case, the exercise was conducted in sub-zero weather in the Vallée Blanche. After building the igloos and seeing that the British officers were safely tucked away for the evening, Jaccoux and a fellow-guide slipped away to a nearby mountain refuge, where they enjoyed a splendid dinner and a comfortable night's sleep. The next day, the *gardien* of the refuge awakened them before dawn, so that they could be present when their students, stiff with cold, emerged from their igloos. In 1959, leaving the Army, he became an *aspirant*, and in 1961 a guide.

It was about three o'clock in the afternoon when Jaccoux and I got back to the Bureau in Chamonix (guides always check in and out of the Bureau, so that Barthélémy will have a record of where everyone is), and as we were leaving he asked me if I would like to come to his house for dinner that

Gaston Rébuffat at work (Dent du Géant in the background).
(Courtesy of P. Tairraz)

evening. I was glad to accept, so he set a time and told me how to get there. He and his first wife, Michèle, and their five-year-old daughter, Claire, were living in a rented chalet on the property of Lionel Terray, who, with Gaston Rébuffat, was the most famous practicing guide in Chamonix. Both were members of the successful French Himalayan expedition to Annapurna in 1950. After their return, Rébuffat and Terray served as active guides with the Syndicat as well as writing and lecturing. Rébuffat, the first man to climb the south face of the Aiguille du Midi, was a prolific mountain photographer and writer and assembled several superb books of photographs. Terray, whose autobiography, *Les Conquérants de l'Inutile*, was something of a best-seller in France, in 1958 helped to make a movie about climbing in Chamonix, *Quand Brillent les Étoiles de Midi*, which many people consider the finest mountain movie ever filmed. Both Terray and Rébuffat became financially successful, and both owned land in the valley—a major ambition of most guides, and a hard one to achieve, since, because of the chancy nature of the guides' employment, French banks will ordinarily not lend them money. Terray had a few cottages on his property, besides a chalet of his own, and the Jaccoux were sharing one of them with another guide and his wife—a couple named Bernezat. The cottage was small, but since the two men were away much of the time during the season, it was a serviceable arrangement for the two wives.

When I arrived at Jaccoux's cottage, after a short but steep walk up from the road, there were already several other guests there. The guides get home so seldom during the season that there is something of a holiday atmosphere around the house when they do. (The Jaccoux customarily spent the late fall in Paris, where they worked as consultants on ski equipment for a sporting-goods store and devoted every free minute to soaking up the theater and music that they had to give up during the season.) As I walked into the small but comfortable upstairs living room—the cottage, like many in the valley, is a two-story affair, with floors that are connected by a trapdoor and a ladder—everyone seemed to be running in and out of the kitchen. Later, I learned that each of the guests had volunteered to cook or bring something for dinner, and this accounted for the activity. (By happy chance, I had brought with me some of the wonderful pâtisserie of the Savoie, which served as dessert.) Jaccoux introduced me to his wife, a tall, very attractive, and extremely energetic blonde. Under her maiden name, Michèle Stamos, she was one of the best-known skiers in France, and at the time Jaccoux met her, she was on the French Olympic team. *"On se rencontrait, on se plaisait, on s'est marié,"* she said. She teaches skiing in the winter, principally to children; she doesn't like to climb, she told me, because she gets frightened. In this she differed from Mme. Bernezat, who is one of the best women climbers in Chamonix and one of the first women to climb the Grand Capucin, a severe, highly technical rock climb in the valley. Surprisingly—or maybe not surprisingly—many women are excellent climbers. Climbing, and especially rock climbing, is not a question of brute strength; balance, agility, and nerve count for a lot more. Mme. Bernezat, a slight, delightfully impish brunette, had just married Bernezat, who that evening was suffering from a severe virus infection. Periodically during dinner, someone would bang an ice axe on the floor, which was just above Bernezat's head, to see whether an answering thump would prove that he was still alive.

Like some of the guides at dinner, Bernezat had an engagement that lasted the whole summer—in his case, teaching climbing to some members of the French Alpine Club. (Altogether, the club has no fewer than fifty thousand members.) The virtue of such an arrangement is that it provides a fixed income for the summer regardless of the weather; in the case of a free-lance guide, a summer of bad weather can reduce him and his family to near starvation. In a good season, on the other hand, free-lance guiding is more profitable, and it also offers a good deal more variety. Moreover, Bernezat was required to spend six weeks or so at a time in various mountain refuges, where his students came for training, while Jaccoux was able to get home almost once a week. In addition to their professional climbing, both Jaccoux and Bernezat went on climbs of their own whenever they could get enough time off. Part of the reputation of a young guide is made by the number of first ascents he has done. Earlier that summer, Bernezat and Lionel Terray had gone to Alaska with a sizable French group to climb Mount Huntington (12,238 feet), and Jaccoux and Bernezat, along with a third guide, did an exceptional first ascent on the south face of the Aiguille du Jardin, near the Aiguille Verte. And during the winter Jaccoux and another guide had done a first ascent of the Aiguille Verte itself by a route that had never been climbed out of season. There are very few firsts left in Chamonix, and it has now become fashionable to do winter climbs of aiguilles that have been climbed many times in the summer.

On the following day, Jaccoux proposed that we go to the Col des Montets to train. The Col des Montets is at the head of the valley near the Swiss border—a lovely forested area from which one gets an entirely novel view of the Chamonix Valley and the mountains, which look remote and almost pastoral. Scattered through the woods are a vast number of boulders about ten feet high. Many of them have been given names—usually after famous aiguilles—and climbers come to practice technique on them. No real damage can be done by a fall or by bad weather, so one can concentrate on form.

On one of the rocks, for example, the whole ascent is done without using one's hands—just on foot traction and balance. Several people were at work when we got there, including a young guide who was practicing on a day off, and a number of very young children from the valley, who were learning to climb. One little boy had his even smaller sister on the end of a climbing rope, and they went up and down the rocks while their mother, sitting casually in the grass below and knitting a sweater, kept saying, *"Tiens bien ta soeur, Jean-Pierre."* Jaccoux and I did some of the standard "routes," and then he and the other guide tried a brief Class VI passage on a boulder. There was nothing at all to hold on to, and the trick consisted of making just the right sequence of moves—and quickly enough so that one did not fall off. After a couple of futile attempts, they quit in disgust.

Later that afternoon, Jaccoux introduced me to one of the instructors at the École Nationale de Ski et d'Alpinisme—André Contamine, one of the crack mountaineers in the region. Contamine had achieved the ultimate distinction possible for a climber in Chamonix today, which is to have a route that he pioneered named after him. In the golden age of the nineteenth century, outstanding climbers had aiguilles named after them, but all the aiguilles have long since been named, so it is only new routes that remain. Contamine and Rébuffat each has a route named after him on the south face of the Aiguille du Midi. Contamine, a slight, intense-looking, intelligent man who was also well known as a photographer, was a teacher at the E.N.S.A. and its predecessor schools for nearly twenty years. The next day, he told us, he was going to take part in examining a hundred and forty *aspirants* to decide which would qualify for the seventy places that were open in the school. The test was going to take three days, and the examiners, he said, would be much more interested in finding candidates who

111

were well founded in every branch of climbing than those who might be sporadically brilliant in one or two techniques. The first day would be a test of physical endurance; each candidate, wearing a large numeral on his back, was to take a four-and-a-half-hour hike carrying about twenty-five pounds—a hike, however, that involved altitude changes of nearly ten thousand feet. The next two days would be devoted to techniques on rock and ice; a candidate had to show absolute mastery of Class IV rock passages and a solid technique on ice. Of the seventy *aspirants* selected, he added, about a third would fail the course.

After talking to Contamine, Jaccoux and I paid a visit to the school itself, which occupies a couple of stone chalet-like structures near the Aiguille du Midi *téléphérique*. The day was Sunday, and not many people were around. In addition to classrooms (in one I noticed an anatomical model used in the first-aid courses), dormitories, and restaurant facilities, the school has an excellent alpine library. On the walls of the main lecture hall were photographs and diagrams of storm formations, avalanches, and the architecture of crevasses. (A good guide can read the snow and detect hidden crevasses, revealed to him by slight discolorations and indentations in the surface.) In the dormitories next door, several *aspirants* were watching a Davis Cup match on television. They were very friendly and greeted Jaccoux warmly; the whole atmosphere was like that of any university just before the beginning of term.

The *aspirants* were, perhaps, somewhat more subdued than usual, for only a few weeks earlier the school had suffered the worst disaster in its history—the accident on the Aiguille Verte—which revealed once again the dangers involved in climbing. The guides are extremely alert to danger in the mountains, of course, and they talk about it among themselves, but they rarely say much about it to clients. I spent the summer of 1964 climbing with Jaccoux, and only once did he announce that a certain passage was going to be dangerous. This occurred toward the end of an all-day climb over terrain that I thought was dangerous but that, from a guide's point of view, was not; at all times during the climb Jaccoux was in an excellent position to arrest any fall. The dangers that worry a guide, and that Jaccoux wanted to call my attention to, are objective dangers—like weather or bad snow conditions. In this case, late in the afternoon, we had to cross a *couloir* down which rocks fell at irregular intervals. (The late afternoon is especially dangerous for rock fall, since the snow that, otherwise, holds the rocks has become melted and unstable.) The route across was very simple, so when Jaccoux announced that the passage was a dangerous one, I was puzzled. He mentioned the rocks, and just then one the size of a football shot down the *couloir.* "*Tu vois le genre,*" he said. I all but flew across. Later, I asked Jaccoux what his general attitude was toward accidents and death in the mountains. He said simply, "*Moi, je suis optimiste.*" The Chamonix guides are, in the main, not very religious in any conventional sense (although Michèle told me that many of the wives are extremely devout), but they have a fatalistic conviction that they will not be hurt. Jaccoux once told me that there are very few guides who have been incapacitated by accidents; either they have no accidents or they are killed. Since the founding of the Syndicat, about one guide a year has lost his life in the mountains, but these accidents have very rarely involved clients; indeed, one can say that there are practically no fatal accidents with clients. Most of the guide accidents occur on rescue missions. I asked Jaccoux whether many clients come to the Bureau claiming to be better alpinists than they are, and then get into trouble because of their inexperience. He said that it usually works the other way—the guides must convince clients that they can really make a climb—although occasionally people who have not climbed in some years return to Chamonix expecting to continue where they left off and try to begin with climbs they cannot manage.

Guides are legally responsible for the safety of their clients, and their authority is absolute when it comes to deciding whether to go on or turn back. Some aspects of their work are fixed by law. For example, the number of climbers on a rope is restricted to two, or sometimes three if the climb is simple enough; on any glacier with crevasses hidden by snow, it is obligatory to rope up; and so on. However, in practice it is all but impossible to follow these rules to the letter; actually, it would be unsafe to do so. Belaying and roping are time-consuming, and although alpine weather usually guarantees one a clear morning, there is an almost inevitable clouding over in the afternoon, and often a storm. Hence, it is very important to be off the mountains as early as possible, and the guide must judge whether the additional safety of a belay is worth the time it takes. Like all first-rate guides before him, Jaccoux has the reputation of being something of a cannon, and on many climbs we found ourselves passing one *cordée* after another. Indeed, one of the main complaints that climbers have about guided climbing is that the guides move too fast, and there is no doubt but that the better the guide the faster he goes. In addition to the safety factor, there is a clear economic reason for this speed. The guide has his schedule of climbs carefully planned over several days, and since they can be practically anywhere in the valley, he simply must get a move on if he is to meet his clients on time and earn his living. Often, a guide who has finished one climb and is in a hurry to keep a second appointment will hand over his clients to another guide for ferrying back to Chamonix.

Because so many climbers, a lot of them inexperienced,

operate without guides in the valley, there are almost daily accidents. To deal with them, an elaborate system, involving four organizations, was worked out.* In the first place, there is the P.S.H.M. (Peloton Spécialisé de Haute Montagne), a unit of the French Army, which has radio or telephone connections with all the mountain refuges near Chamonix. Some of the men in the outfit have guide status, and all are specially trained in rescue work. In addition, the P.S.H.M. has two large military helicopters, which are kept in the valley from June 15th until September 1st. Every request for help or rescue goes first to the unit's headquarters, which occupy the second floor of a Shell service station near the Chamonix railroad terminal. Except during the month of August, the next step is for the P.S.H.M. to get in touch with the Guide Bureau, where it becomes the responsibility of the Chef des Guides to organize the rescue team. This generally consists of one or two guides and a group of military personnel, who are flown as close as possible to the accident. During the month of August, which is the heart of the season, the role of the guides is taken over for two weeks by the instructors at the E.N.S.A., and for two weeks by the instructors at the military alpine school. This is so the guides can have a solid month free for work. Barthélémy told me that before this system was inaugurated, August had been a nightmare, with the guides almost constantly out on rescue work. He showed me a remarkable handwritten log, going back to the last century, of rescues that guides had participated in. Some of the pre-helicopter ones involved caravans of ten or fifteen men, who often had to climb for hours to get even within sight of the accident; now the helicopter does most of the work, and does it much more quickly and safely. A helicopter rescue is an extremely expensive business,

---

* All of this has now been replaced by a specially trained unit of the French police who are responsible for rescues on a full-time basis.

however, and many climbers carry accident insurance to help pay its cost.

I had an unexpected opportunity to see the rescue system in action. One Sunday morning in August, I was in the Bureau talking to Barthélémy when a woman came in, obviously very distraught. She said that her husband, who was an expert climber with Himalayan experience, had set out on Thursday night with some friends to climb the Grépon by a very difficult route. He had told her to expect them back on Friday or, if the weather was bad—which it had been— by Saturday. It was now Sunday morning, and he had not returned. Barthélémy told her to go at once to the P.S.H.M. and report to them. I followed along behind, and by the time I got there, the woman had already left a careful description of her husband's route and party with the officer in charge. He was in a room filled with radios and telephones over the garage, relaying the message to one of the helicopters, which was then circling the mountains on routine patrol duty. The helicopter flew over the Grépon and followed the route along the glacier where the missing men should have been; we could see it through the window of the office as we listened to the pilot's radio report. He spotted three men on the glacier, verified that they matched the description of the missing climbers, and reported that they were in good shape. The officer in charge then relayed the news to the climber's wife.

Most of the accidents in Chamonix—though certainly not all—can be traced back to sheer folly on the part of the climbers involved. This was brought home to me only too vividly one weekend in August. Because the weather had been dubious, Jaccoux and I had called off a climb of Mont Blanc and decided, instead, to do Mont Blanc du Tacul, a neighboring peak that is readily accessible from the top of the Aiguille du Midi *téléphérique*. In the morning, we took the six o'clock car to the top, and as we walked across the glacier to the base of the mountain, it became evident that the weather was going to get worse. Still, Jaccoux was convinced that we had enough time for the climb, so we started off. We got to the top just as a kind of light hail or corn snow began falling. "*Grésil*," Jaccoux said, and proposed that we get back down as quickly as possible, because it was now going to snow in earnest. By the time we reached the base of the mountain, our tracks of the morning were hidden under a thick layer of heavy snow. We ourselves were out of danger then, but in the next half hour, as we made our way back across the glacier to the *téléphérique*, we witnessed several acts of almost total brainlessness on the part of climbers in the area. First, we spotted a climber wandering around all by himself on the glacier; Jaccoux hailed him, and we tied him onto our rope. He had been with another party on the Tacul, and halfway up, having got tired, he had decided to stop where he was and wait for his group to pick him up on their way back. This would have been all right, except that when it began to snow, he had started out for the *téléphérique* on his own. Not only was this a foolish thing to do on a heavily crevassed glacier but he had lost his sense of direction, and when we encountered him, he was heading across the Vallée Blanche in the direction of Italy over very dangerous terrain. The three of us had not gone far when we saw two climbers ascending the very difficult and by now extremely slippery rock of the south face of the Aiguille du Midi, despite the obviously deteriorating weather. When Jaccoux studied them through his field glasses, he discovered that one of them was climbing up La Voie Contamine and the other La Voie Rébuffat, with the rope between them stretched out horizontal and providing no security at all. (Later, another guide told us that one of the men had slipped and swung like a gigantic pendulum on the rope, which had

The ridge between the Aiguille du Midi and the Aiguille du Plan. (Courtesy of P. Tairraz)

miraculously caught on an outcropping, and that it was only good fortune that had permitted the two of them to get back to the valley.) Then, when we reached the *téléphérique* station, someone shouted to Jaccoux that a group of people without a rope, and without crampons or any other snow or ice equipment, had decided to walk along the ridge that goes from the Aiguille du Midi to the Aiguille du Plan. From this ridge, which is in many places just about wide enough for one foot at a time, there is a drop of several thousand feet on each side. Jaccoux looked at them through his field glasses and, shaking his head in angry disbelief, confirmed the report, but there was nothing he could do to stop them. (We had ourselves been over the ridge a few days before and had passed a *cordée* in which the second man, who was obviously having great difficulty, turned out to be wearing light *après-ski* shoes, with soles like tennis sneakers.) These people, too, were lucky and somehow got back safely, but the P.S.H.M. gets at least two calls a day during the season concerning people who are not lucky.

Jaccoux has complete confidence in himself in the mountains. He told me that he never relies on the rope for security in any passage less than Class V in difficulty; he has an absolute faith that nothing will happen to him. (Michèle told me that he refuses to wear one of the plastic helmets, like a miner's, that are now rather widely favored in Chamonix for warding off falling rocks; if one feels the need to climb in a suit of armor, he says, one might as well not climb at all. It is a faith that he manages to communicate to his family and, certainly, to his clients. Once, when I said that a climb Jaccoux had proposed might be too difficult for me, he said, simply, "You'll be with me." We did the climb. But it is one thing to act and another to wait, and Michèle and the other wives do not have it easy. During the season, the guides work every day except in bad weather and on August 15th, which is *la fête des guides* in Chamonix—an all-day affair that starts at nine in the morning with the laying of a wreath on a monument in the Chamonix cemetery to the guides who have died while climbing. It is one of the rare times during the year when the whole Syndicat is assembled, and last year's wreath-laying was especially meaningful in view of the accident on the Aiguille Verte. At a few minutes before nine, the guides assembled in the square in front of the cemetery, all dressed in their formal climbing costume of dark brown. (Dufour, whom I spotted in the crowd, said, "*Nous sommes très folkloriques aujourd'hui.*") The cemetery contains the grave of Whymper, along with the graves of many hundreds of other climbers and skiers. Some of the tombstones are in the form of the aiguille on which the climber was killed, and some are adorned with carvings of mountain ropes or axes or skis. The ceremony was brief and poignant, and when it was over, everyone moved along to the monument in the center of town that honors Balmat. Another wreath was laid here, and then the crowd went on to the courtyard in front of the church for the traditional blessing of the guides' ropes and ice axes by M. l'Archiprêtre de Chamonix. The priest gave his blessing and commented on the accident on the Aiguille Verte and on the pleasures and dangers of climbing, and then the crowd went inside for Mass. That afternoon, many of us went to Les Gaillands and paid a small fee to watch the guides give a traditional demonstration of the art of rock climbing. Climbs of every degree of difficulty were done before a crowd of nearly four thousand, and the show ended with a magnificent display of rappelling by a group of about ten guides. The proceeds went to the guides' accident fund, which Barthélémy said is now just big enough to pay a few thousand dollars to the family of any guide who is killed.

The next morning, the sky was overcast, so Jaccoux proposed a trip down the valley to Argentière to pay a call on the famous retired guide Armand Charlet. Charlet, who came from a family celebrated in the annals of guiding, was a link between the present generation of guides and the great guides of the nineteenth century. Although he was too young—he was born in 1900—to have known Whymper, he grew up in an atmosphere where Whymper's exploits were household words, and he remembers seeing Whymper's daughter having tea in one of the mountain refuges. His entire life was spent in the mountains, where, among other achievements, he made ninety-two ascents of the Aiguille Verte, some of them by new routes. He was an absolute master of technique on ice, and there are many wonderful photographs showing him walking up a vertical ice wall as if it were a sidewalk in Chamonix. He taught at the E.N.S.A.

Armand Charlet.
(Courtesy of Emile Gos)

for a while, and in recent years had the job of inspecting the various mountain refuges around the valley—a job that calls for a good deal of hiking and climbing. Jaccoux and I found him in front of the Argentière guide bureau (the guides of Argentière are nominally part of the Chamonix Syndicat, but they operate autonomously), and I was immediately taken by him. He was a man of immense character, dignity, and intelligence. He was once regarded by his colleagues as something of a loner—*"un fou,"* as he put it—because he did not stick to the usual routine of the guides of that time, and he was often accused of monopolizing all the really skilled clients. Actually, Charlet said, it was the other way around—he simply concentrated on developing a client from a beginner to an expert, and as the client got better, he was naturally able to go on more difficult and, from the guide's point of view, more profitable climbs. In Charlet's heyday, climbing without a guide was a rarity, while now it is commonplace. People then took guides even on the simplest walks, which meant that a guide could earn a living without having any real mountaineering skill. Today, things have changed. The simpler climbs are usually done without guides, and an experienced climber who takes a guide does so, as one of them told me, only for *"une très grande course."* Chamonix guides are frequently hired for climbs elsewhere in Europe, and many Swiss and Italian guides bring clients into the valley; the circle of crack climbing guides is fairly small, and they all tend to know one another. Jaccoux feels that the guides are now by all odds the best climbers in Europe, which was not always the case.

Charlet invited us to his house for a drink. He lived in a chalet that dates back to the eighteenth century and was filled with climbing mementos. After looking at a photograph of him doing an ice climb, I asked him whether he had some secret technique, and he told me that it was all in his ankles, which were exceptionally strong. And indeed they were; in the photograph his feet were bent up to form an almost impossible angle with his legs. As we were leaving, Jaccoux asked Charlet for a suggestion as to what we might do in such weather, and Charlet suggested some ice training at the Glacier des Bossons.

Ice is a medium completely different from rock. It is, in my opinion, a hostile world. Ice climbing is largely a matter of balance and footwork, and the main weapons are crampons and an ice axe. The axe is helpful in maintaining one's balance, and it is also used for chopping out steps, if necessary; the object is to cut as few steps as possible, since this is an extremely tiring business, and also very slow. Then the climber must learn the technique of *cramponnage*—walking with crampons. The entire trick consists of keeping one's

foot parallel to the ice face, with all the points of the crampons dug in; obviously, the steeper the ice the more one has
to bend one's ankles, so when Charlet said that his secret
was strong ankles he was being completely accurate. My
own ankles are nothing special, and I found learning to use
crampons extremely painful. The Glacier des Bossons, a
steep, highly crevassed glacier that comes down almost into
the valley, is an ideal place to practice ice climbing, since it
offers passages that are quite difficult but not too long. We
spent a couple of hours fighting our way up the glacier while
Jaccoux told me, in very precise terms, what he thought of
my inability to hang on. Though I didn't know it, the entire
epic struggle was witnessed from below by a large group of
tourists, and when we were coming down, I heard someone
say, "One of them looked as if he knew what he was doing,
and the other didn't."

By the end of the season, Jaccoux and I had climbed
sample aiguilles all over the valley, and I felt I had begun to
get the hang and the flavor of the thing. Some of our climbs
involved spending the night in one of the mountain refuges,
which range from near-hotels that serve four-course meals
and can accommodate two hundred climbers to small huts
that can shelter only a few climbers at a time. In the larger
ones, the ambience is immensely cheerful and the views are
magnificent. Many can be reached by trails, and often entire
families with children come up to spend the night just to see
the sun rise. There is a great deal of chatter, wine drinking,
and mild horseplay. At sundown, however, everyone turns
in, because the climbs from the refuges usually begin very
early—at one or two o'clock in the morning. Climbers of all
ages and sexes sleep jumbled up in big dormitory-like
rooms, but usually everybody is so exhausted that wakeful-
ness is no problem.

One day at the very end of the summer, Michèle tele-
phoned me to say that Jaccoux had a sore throat and would

probably be out of action for a few days. I asked her how he had got it, and she told me a remarkable and disturbing tale. Jaccoux had been hired by the French Alpine Club to help a group of its members make repairs on the Vallot hut, which is near the top of Mont Blanc. The work party was to be flown up by commercial plane and landed on a snow plateau near the hut. (Touring the aiguilles in light planes is now something of a fad in Chamonix. I was told of a climber who, during an attempt on Mont Blanc, was overcome near the Vallot by altitude sickness. He was so determined to complete the climb, however, that he later hired a plane to fly him and a guide back to the Vallot, from which they finished the ascent. Afterward, they were chauffeured back to the valley.) Jaccoux took the job because he was curious about the flight. The whole operation was supposed to last only a couple of hours, but the work took longer than expected, and when it came time to go down, the pilot refused to make more than one trip. This meant leaving some of the club members at the Vallot hut, and since Jaccoux felt that he could not safely do this, he took them to the next refuge below. Here they could have spent the night comfortably, but Jaccoux had an important appointment in Chamonix, and it looked as if he were going to miss it. Finally, he decided to go back down to Chamonix at once, rather than spend the night in the refuge. He told the Alpine Club people that he would look after them on the way down if they wanted to come, but that he could not be responsible for them, since they were too many for one guide to handle legally. They decided to come with him anyway. Then, on the way down, they were caught in a small avalanche. Only some very fast maneuvering by Jaccoux saved them from being swept away, and he arrived back in Chamonix tired and suffering a bit from exposure. His sore throat was the result.

* * *

On my final day in Chamonix, Jaccoux invited me to a monumental community lunch. (I brought seventeen pastries.) The season was nearly over. Snow had already covered the tops of the aiguilles, and they sparkled in the special clear light of early autumn. Bernezat and his wife were together for almost the first time since his illness. Guides and their wives and girl friends were dropping in all afternoon. It was a happy and sentimental time for everybody, and a few days later, when I was back in Geneva, I phoned the Guide Bureau to thank Jaccoux for everything. When he got on the phone, he sounded exhausted. He said he had just come back from a rescue mission, but he didn't seem to want to talk about it, so after sending my love to Michèle and Claire, I said goodbye. That afternoon, *Le Dauphiné-Libéré*, a newspaper that covers Savoie, carried a short paragraph:

> The rescuers who on Thursday, at the end of the afternoon, went in search of Claude Aker, who fell on the eastern spur of Mont Maudit, had a moment of great suspense. In order to speed their ascent, the guides Martinetti and Claude Jaccoux took an ice *couloir* almost parallel to the rock *couloir* where the accident occurred. Suddenly there was an avalanche of giant ice blocks that passed very close, but fortunately it did not hit the members of the rescue team. They went on to discover the body of Claude Aker about five hundred meters above the glacier. On Friday morning, two helicopter flights were made to bring the guides, together with the body of the victim, back to Chamonix. At eleven o'clock, the operation was completed.

A rescue like this—though this one was perhaps more dangerous than most—is part of a guide's life. Jaccoux, like most guides, does not covet danger simply for the sake of danger, although the alternation of hope and fear, the difficulties of climbing, the awareness of the beauty of the mountains, and the satisfaction that comes from teaching other people to do something that one loves to do oneself make him determined to spend his life as a guide. Guides are not supermen. They work hard for a living and are subject to the same human weaknesses as anyone else, but the very nature of their craft—its closeness to danger and, often, death, and the enormous responsibilities involved—gives them a strength and dignity. One evening when Barthélémy and I were watching the Syndicat assemble for the *tour de rôle*, he said to me, half in jest and half in earnest, *"Ces types-là, ils sont des purs."*

4

Two Days in the Life of a Member of the French Alpine Club

Glaciers often make groaning sounds from their depths as they move, like elderly people coming down flights of stairs, and one of the crevasses moans slightly as I step forward. This seems to me—standing there on a tiny, sharp ice ridge leading between two monster crevasses high in the French Alps—like a bad omen, and I retreat. While I am thinking what to do next, I have the sudden conviction that of all the fifty thousand members in good standing of the French Alpine Club I am the most chicken. This goad works to the extent that I try the ridge again, starting with the other foot. I now begin to wonder what will happen if I slip. This reflection is needless, for clearly what will happen is that I will fall into the bottom of one of the crevasses. No doubt climbing is somewhat crazy, but there is a profound satisfaction in conquering one's deepest fears, a sort of spiritual satisfaction which in this age of televised and predigested experience is all but disappearing. Let me go back to the beginning of the day.

We are late. We are always late. Jaccoux somehow manages to arrive three seconds before the last train or *téléphérique* or something. It's not that we will miss the last train— the cog railroad that goes from Chamonix to Montenvers, a vantage point above the Mer de Glace glacier, at 6,300 feet. There are trains until nearly 6 P.M. But from Montenvers we still have a four-hour climb to the Couvercle climbing refuge which sits beyond the head of the glacier at about 8,800 feet. I figure that if we are on the glacier at five we will have about two and a half hours of light, and the thought of groping around the moraine with flashlights does not appeal to me very much. Just in case, I check that my flashlight is actually working. A few years ago I went with a group up to the Couvercle, without Jaccoux, at night and in a rainstorm. It turned out that everyone had forgotten his flashlight except me. But I had not checked to see if mine was working. It was not, and by the time we found our way to the Couvercle in a raging storm, it was close to midnight. Well, at least my flashlight works now.

There is Jaccoux, racing up in his orange Fiat with Colette, who in a gesture of loyalty has decided to come along. Colette is wearing a pair of modish, off-orange knickerbockers and a matching riding jacket with a yellow scarf. She looks as if she is dressed for golf. I hope she has a sweater at least. Jaccoux unloads his sixty- or seventy-pound *sac du guide* which contains, among other things, two climbing ropes, some pitons, a hammer, several small rope slings, a pair of crampons, a first-aid kit complete with Alka

Seltzer—Jaccoux is a bit fragile of liver—two pipes, some reading material, two flashlights (no fool he) and some extra warm clothing.

I have my sack which includes, in addition to my crampons and down jacket, my red plastic helmet for warding off falling stones and food for the expedition. The last two items have been a source of irritation. Jaccoux refuses to wear a helmet and I refuse *not* to wear one. He has several interesting rationalizations for his attitude, the latest being that it cuts down his vision. My own rationalization is very simple. I do not want to get hit on the head by a rock. As for the food, in guided climbing, at least in the French Alps, it is the client who supplies the food—and carries it, I might add. I am usually too nervous while climbing to eat and therefore have a tendency either to forget completely about buying any, or if I don't forget, to get some sort of salami which Jaccoux says is bad for his liver. On one notable occasion when I forgot to bring food, Jaccoux sat down in the snow and refused to move. We were saved by the appearance of a large party of climbers who had an extra bar of chocolate. This time I have *two* different types of salami and four bars of chocolate. Still, my provisioning compares unfavorably with the *nourriture* supplied by the rest of Jaccoux's clientele, most notably a Parisienne who usually turns up with shrimp canapes, paté du foie, and the like. At least we will eat. What Colette has in her *sac* I hesitate to think.

We are on the train. Apart from us, there is a straggle of tourists who will catch a ten-minute view of the glacier before coming back down. Some may even be planning to spend the night at the Hotel de Montenvers, an ancient solid stone affair now being run and renovated by a young French couple—the Remi de Vivis. In its present guise the hotel offers fine food, a marvelous glacial panorama, and the *coupe perrichon glace myrtille et vanille fruits vodka*. This last is a

129

delicious vanilla ice cream sundae filled with fresh fruits, smothered in whipped cream and laced with vodka. Staggering down the Mer de Glace, more dead than alive, I have often been sustained by the vision of a *coupe perrichon*, or perhaps two, which await me if I can just gather enough energy to climb the last set of metal ladders that lead off the glacier and up to the trail that goes to the hotel. Now, I am suddenly seized by the manic notion that we should simply abandon the horrible four-hour climb to the refuge and stay the night at the hotel feasting off *coupe perrichons*!

This fantasy is reinforced by the sight of Abigail, Remi de Vivi's wife, at the Montenvers station. She is seeing someone off to Chamonix, and she invites all of us to a feast at the hotel. I would accept instantly, but I know that Jaccoux is determined to climb *something* tomorrow and the only climbs accessible from the hotel are more difficult than the one we had planned. Jaccoux mutters something about staying at the hotel and doing the Brioche de l'M the next day, a ghastly route on the Aiguelle de l'M which, according to rumor, features some sort of passage of V on slick rock covered with lichen. The prospect of having to slither up lichen after a night of feasting at the hotel is too much for me, and after a certain amount of grumbling from Jaccoux, we head toward the glacier.

We have descended the ladders and are now on the glacier. The Mer de Glace is an amiable old iceflow, creased with crevasses especially at the bottom end. In the winter, hundreds of people ski down the glacier, and in the summer hundreds of people, probably thousands, trudge up it. The various organizations in Chamonix responsible for the safety of climbers mark the route on the glacier with large painted metal barrels.

Toward the top there are several routes leading to various climbing refuges and each route is marked with barrels of different colors. The barrels leading to the Couvercle are painted yellow, and I can see them strung out along the glacier in a reassuring—more or less—straight line. In fact, I am beginning to feel a virtuous sense of self-satisfaction when I encounter a totally unexpected obstacle—this pair of crevasses with the tiny ice ridge leading between them. Jaccoux and Colette, having somehow negotiated the ridge, are comfortably settled on the other side. I have been over the glacier a week or so before but have no recollection of any such ice ridge. It occurs to me that Jaccoux might have taken some sort of shortcut, but just behind him, there is one of the infernal yellow barrels. Glaciers change so quickly that the damn ridge must have formed in the last few days.

I put a foot tentatively on the ridge, and this is the moment at which I hear the glacier groan and quickly retreat. Overcoming my fears, I step forward again. I now remember something my father once said to me: "You don't have to be crazy to climb mountains. But it helps!" I again retreat. Jaccoux, who has been watching this charade with a growing sense of impatience in view of the hour—it is now well after six—has bestirred himself and is now working his way back across the ridge, knocking sizable pieces off of the top of it with his ice axe and muttering, "*Quel métier!*" The now-crenelated ridge looks reasonably inviting, and I make my way over it.

Like a rocket, Jaccoux has taken off up the glacier with Colette gamely trying to keep up. I am content to amble along at my own pace—we are not roped since all of the crevasses in the upper part of the glacier are small and clearly visible. The sun has set and the moon is doing its best to chin itself on the Col des Hirondelles, a break in the range of mountains that demarcate the Franco-Italian border. A few clouds, born in the chill of the night air, cling to the vertical architecture of the *aiguilles*. Tomorrow we are

The Aiguilles of Chamonix. (Courtesy of Gaston Rébuffat)

going to traverse the needle of the Nun. To the left of the Mer de Glace as we go up is a wall of *aiguilles* which have all been given ecclesiastic titles—the Monk, the Nun, the Bishop, and so on. The summit of the Nun is at 11,022 feet, a small alp, and by Chamonix standards it is not much of a climb. However, we have had two weeks of really bad weather, and everything higher is pretty thoroughly plastered in snow.

It is now quite dark and we are picking our way through the upper moraine with flashlights. Soon we find the *egralets*, a series of ladders, ramps, and rock passages with footholds that have been cut out of the rock leading vertically up the trail to the Couvercle. By the time we reach the trail it is pitch black and we are all sufficiently winded to stop for a breather and a swig of tea from my canteen. After a brisk walk of a half-hour or so by flashlight, we can see the lights of the refuge above us. In the dark it looks like an ocean liner in a sea of snow. It is a friendly and reassuring sight. The Couvercle is built of solid stone bricks, and during the height of the climbing season—July 1–September 1—it can, and often does, accommodate more than 250 climbers in several large dormitories. Simple but good meals are served, and the place is constantly being resupplied by porters and helicopters from the Chamonix Valley at relatively low cost, considering the effort it takes to bring the food up. It is now past the climbing season, and as we enter the main dining room there are perhaps forty people in it. Most of them, it turns out, are young *aspirants guides* (apprentice guides) who are in the process of taking their final examinations on snow and rock from the instructors of the École Nationale de Ski et d'Alpinisme, who will decide whether or not they qualify as full-fledged guides.

There is a good deal of red wine being passed around among the *aspirants* and they look as if they are out on a pleasant excursion rather than taking an examination. The thought crosses my mind that it might be an ideal time to have an accident, if one is going to have one, considering the force that is assembled for a potential rescue.

Through the murk of pipe and cigarette smoke I make out the familiar craggy features of Gerard Herzog. Gerard is the brother of Maurice Herzog, the man who led the French expedition that climbed Annapurna in Nepal. Gerard, now in his fifties, is one of the best climbers in France. He is a writer and television producer and his wife José, an actress and singer, is one of the most beautiful women I have ever seen. Happily, José is also there; not only that, they have an enormous vat of delicately seasoned noodles which they offer to share with us. We order a couple of bottles of wine—this is, after all, France, and no climb in the Alps is complete without a good dose of red wine. Gerard and José are planning to do a long snow climb, but after several glasses of wine, the ambience has become such that they too decide to climb the Nun, and, it appears, so have a large contingent of *aspirants* and instructors. By ten the wine has been exhausted, and we turn into our bunks for a few hours of sleep.

It is 3:00 A.M. The guardian of the refuge has just turned on the lights in our dormitory. It is freezing cold and my first thought is that perhaps there is a terrible storm outside and I can go back to sleep. I peer tentatively out a window. Stars and planets are flickering brightly in the night sky—no storm. "*Les étoiles,* Jaccoux," I announce. Jaccoux replies indistinctly, attempting to escape the grisly implications of my discovery by burying himself deeper in his blankets. Gerard stirs, and soon the five of us are groping our way downstairs to breakfast. The night before Jaccoux had decided that we had two alternatives: to get up very early to try to beat the *aspirants* to the Nun and avoid being showered by rocks from above; or to wait until the *aspirants* had climbed the Nun and were moving onto the Bishop. We have opted for the latter, since it is hopeless to try to beat the *aspirants* who are all young and strong and will be moving like crazy. This has given us an extra hour to sleep. Breakfast consists of thick fresh bread with jam and honey and coffee with milk and sugar. We will have lunch on the Nun.

By the time we leave the Couvercle the sky has turned the clear, pastel blue of the early dawn of a lovely day. Our route leads up the snowfields back of the Couvercle. The snow is hard as rock and we have put on our crampons, which in the snow make the crunching sound of someone eating corn on the cob. Colette has somehow lost a crampon. It has fallen off in the snow. By the time we recover it and she is shoed up again, we have all had a splendid and welcome fifteen-minute rest. By now the sun is beginning to come up in earnest, and the red rock of the *aiguilles* is bathed in a rosy glow. We can see various groups of *aspirants* on several rock faces shouting instructions to each other. We climb a very steep snow slope and come to rest on a somewhat precarious-looking tongue of snow which abuts the rock ribs of the Nun. Jaccoux and Gerard take their ropes out of their sacks, and we rope up in groups of three and two. Jaccoux takes a last puff on a cigarette and then launches himself onto the rock. He disappears, leaving only a trail of red rope. *"A toi,"* I hear him say from somewhere. I give my plastic helmet a final reassuring twist, and after a few abortive flapping motions against the rock, begin to climb. It is not very difficult, but I try to be careful not to dislodge any loose stones on my friends.

I reach Jaccoux, who has now lit his pipe and is calmly puffing away on a narrow rock ledge. He has wound the rope around a protruding rock, and as I move up, he coils the extra rope in a neat pile on the ledge. To save time he will move up to the next ledge, from which he can secure me while I protect Colette. To make sure that nothing goes wrong, Jaccoux fastens me to a rock with a rope sling so that even if Colette should fall, there is no way that she—and the rest of us—can become detached from the Nun. Colette is climbing slowly but well, and while I am coiling in the rope leading from me to her, I have a minute to look up and catch a glimpse of the last of the *aspirants* disappearing along a ridge well above.

The five of us move steadily up the Nun like a quintuped attached together by nerves of red rope. Just below the summit we reach the only really difficult passage—a delicate blade of smooth rock which juts precariously over the glacier a few thousand feet below. The smooth surface of the blade is broken by a few small indentations that will have to serve as footholds. Eight feet or so up the blade I can see a piton, a metal wedge driven into a crack and left there permanently, glinting in the sun. Jaccoux heads up the rock in the direction of the piton. Good climbers always manage to stay away from the rock with their bodies so that their center of gravity is directly above their feet, thus imparting the greatest possible traction to the rubber soles of their climbing shoes. Jaccoux is a master at this technique, and when he climbs a rock face, he gives one the impression that he is going up a ladder with deep rungs. When I try it myself I usually find that the "rungs" are almost imperceptible indentations in the rock to which his feet have somehow adhered. Jaccoux has reached the piton. He takes a metal ring with a snap that opens by pressing on it—a carabiner—from a collection that he has been carrying like cartridges on a rope sling over his shoulder. The piton has a hole in the end protruding from the rock, and Jaccoux snaps his carabiner into it and then runs the rope through the fastener into the carabiner, which snaps shut with a click. Now he is protected from below, since should he fall, his drop will be stopped by the rope attached to the piton. He continues up, reaches the summit, and settles himself into a place where he can watch the rest of us ascend.

I press a toe against the slab and, by wrapping part of an arm over a ledge, manage to move my foot into another minuscule indentation. I now see that by stretching my leg and pushing against the edge of the slab I can maneuver myself into a position from which I can make a lunge for the piton.

Holding on to pitons is considered bad form but, as I see it, it beats falling. Now, by pushing off against the piton, I succeed in reaching a rock ledge that leads directly to the summit. During the course of all this I have managed to cut a finger and it is bleeding generously. José, who is slithering her way up the slab, shouts up to me not to worry about it as she will fix everything at the summit. The summit is a tiny

Gaston Rébuffat climbing a smooth vertical wall, Chamonix.
(Courtesy of Gaston Rébuffat)

point barely capable of holding us all—hanging from it in different directions. José bandages my finger, and as she does so, she says, "Where but in France could you find a beautiful woman on the summit of the Nun to heal your finger?" It is a fine sentiment, and, somewhat winded, I settle down on a rock finger to have lunch in the bright sun.

It is very important to avoid being out in the Alps in the late afternoon. The weather turns bad and the snow melts on the glaciers, opening the crevasses. What is a safe romp on the frozen snow in the morning can become a dangerous nightmare in the afternoon. So after a quick lunch we head down. Descending is harder, at least for most people, myself included, than going up. It is difficult to maintain the right balance and get the necessary traction. Also, one is much more conscious of height. On the other hand, there is the consoling thought that each rope length brings one closer to home, i.e., the Couvercle. The first passage leading off of the Nun is a rappel. In a rappel one loops the rope between one's legs, around the back and over a shoulder. It is easier to carry out than to describe. The net effect is that one can then slide down the rope using the feet as guides along the wall. It is as if one were walking down the wall under the control of the rope. (In fact, there is so much friction from the rope that gloves must be worn, and, after a certain amount of experience, I have taken to wearing leather-lined pants.) It is a generally safe procedure provided that the rappel rope has been carefully placed and provided that there is a good terrace to land on below. It requires, above all, willing suspension of disbelief, since the walls one goes down are usually absolutely vertical.

In any case, Jaccoux goes first, protected by Gerard with a security rope. Having two strong climbers with us, we enjoy the luxury of being able to send Jaccoux down to look for a landing place, with Gerard securing the rope. If Gerard had not been along, I would have gone first. Jaccoux disappears completely, and after a few minutes it is Colette's turn. As we watch, from above, she disappears over a rock and after a minute or so it is clear from what she is shouting that she is in serious trouble.

Not being able to see her, there is nothing to do but to let her down on the rope like a package. Gerard calls, telling her to use her feet against the rock as much as possible. Then, as the rope tightens around his back, he lets her down foot by foot while José and I try to do whatever we can to help. After a few anxious minutes, the rope becomes slack and we know she is down. Next, it is my turn.

The first step of the rappel is the hardest for me. One must give up the security of a comfortable ledge and go over the edge straight down, facing in toward the rock. I take a step or two down the wall with the rope sliding around my back. I look down and my heart sinks. Below there is nothing. No wonder Colette panicked. The rock face simply disappears below the overhang from which we have been rappeling. Jaccoux shouts up that everything is all right and tells me to simply put my weight on the rope and let go. Gerard calls down with reassurance. Knowing that there is no choice and that I must keep my nerves under control, I take a deep breath and swing backwards on the rope. For an instant I dangle in midair but then the rope swings me back against the face below, and after what seems like a lifetime I can feel my feet back on the rock and can walk down the rest of the face. I feel an enormous sense of relief and elation. José and Gerard rappel down with no trouble at all. From our ledge we can see that the summit of the Nun looks like a perfect rock *capuchon*—a Nun's bonnet. Jaccoux leads us skillfully from ledge to ledge downward to the glacier below.

By the time we reach it the hard snow of the morning has turned to the consistency of cream soup, and I slosh and slide my way back to the Couvercle a bit behind the others. They are sunning themselves on the terrace of the refuge, and Colette and José, brown in the sun, look like fashion models from *Elle*. I stop for a brief drink and head for the Mer de Glace. Jaccoux and Colette are staying at the Couvercle since he has another client coming up from the valley to meet him there. Gerard and José will come down later, and I

Claude Jaccoux negotiating an overhang, Chamonix.
(Photograph © 1978, Gianfranco Gorgoni/CONTACT)

am happy to be alone with my thoughts. It is a glorious afternoon. Wildflowers peer timidly from behind patches of light snow. Streams of clear water are falling onto the glacier. I stop on a rock and the entire group of *aspirants* passes me running, literally bounding from rock to rock, on their way down to the valley. Crowds of guides and tourists make their way up the glacier, and by four in the afternoon I am at the ladders leading to the Hotel Montenvers and the *coupe perrichon*. As I stop and look out over the great walls of the French Alps, it occurs to me that never have I felt more alive or happier.

5

On Vous Cherche

The summer of 1971 in the Alps was one of the best in recent years—day after day of nearly perfect cloudless, sunny weather. It was also one of the worst—perhaps the worst ever—from the point of view of alpine accidents. By the end of August, in the region of Mont Blanc alone, there had been 77 deaths attributed to climbing or walking in the mountains, and 120 reported accidents involving injuries. (These were presumably injuries that were serious enough to involve some sort of mountain rescue, since minor injuries are not reported at all.) The good weather, ironically, was in part responsible for this perhaps record toll, since more people were climbing in the region than ever before. Many of these climbers were very young, and many were almost completely inexperienced and unaware of the dangers that are an inevitable part of high alpine climbing—sudden changes of weather, hidden crevasses, and, in dry weather, excessive rockfall. As if to epitomize the tragic aspect of the season, an incident took place at the end of the summer which not only resulted in the deaths of two inexperienced climbers (seven others were hospitalized with varying degrees of frostbite) but revived a demand that has been made in the past in France: that some sort of legal restrictions be placed on climbers and what they are allowed to climb.

During the last week in August, a group of eleven young people—mostly teen-agers—arrived in Chamonix with a young counselor from a nearby summer camp where they had been vacationing. The counselor had some alpine experience but was not a qualified professional guide, and none of the young people had had any real mountain experience at all. Early in the week, they hiked up to a refuge cabin, and on Thursday they set off to climb—or so it seems, since after the accident there were conflicting reports as to what they *had* intended to do—the Aiguille du Tour, one of the easiest snow-and-rock climbs in the Chamonix region, but still a climb that requires care. Somehow, they found themselves on the wrong peak, and then were hit by a sudden and violent mountain storm. An experienced group would have kept moving, and, in any case, would have had suitable clothing and extra food for such an emergency. Most of these campers had, at best, light summer jackets, and there was no emergency food and no water and no equipment for melting snow. Freezing, they stopped where they were, and it was not until early the next morning that some members of the group were able to get down to the refuge, where there was telephone communication with the valley, and where, fortunately, five guides had been spending the night in preparation for their own climbs. With the help of a

143

mountain-rescue helicopter, the guides were able to get most of the party back down to Chamonix, but not before two boys, seventeen years old and twenty-one years old, had died from exposure. It was noted after the accident that such a party should have taken at least three, and possibly four, professional guides. It was also noted that this would have cost the hikers something like two hundred dollars in guides' fees, which they could not have afforded. However, as someone remarked, "Would you allow a bunch of children with no experience and no safety equipment to go automobile racing just because they felt like doing it?"

This incident, and some of the other accidents that took place during the summer, inevitably reminded people in Chamonix of the extraordinary series of alpine accidents and rescues that took place during the famous 1965 and 1966 climbing seasons, some of which involved combinations of bad fortune, disparate personalities, courage and cowardice, generosity and avarice, put together in juxtapositions that resembled the fabric of a great, if implausible, novel. In June of that second season, a distinguished French climber, Pierre Henry, assembled some statistics on climbing accidents in the French Alps and published them in *La Montagne*, the journal of the French Alpine Club. These statistics could be gathered precisely, since rescue work there is a police function (with the help of local Guide Bureaus and the like), and accidents in the mountains, like automobile accidents, are subject to full police inquiry. Every year between 1962 and 1965, M. Henry reported, there were between 150 and 180 accidents (some involving more than one person) in the mountains of France. These annually required the intervention of from twelve hundred to two thousand rescuers and from three hundred to five hundred helicopter flights, and each year about sixty deaths resulted from these accidents. (During the same period, there was an average of eighty climbing deaths a year in the Swiss Alps, and of twenty-five a year in Britain.)* In a breakdown of these statistics, M. Henry disclosed that in an average year about 75 percent of the accidents occur in good weather, and that about 40 percent are due to simple falls, the rest being divided up among avalanches, crevasses, lightning (which claims one or two victims a year), and the like. The proportion of accidents decreases with the difficulty of the climb—reflecting the fact that only very good climbers can do difficult climbing. (Their accidents, however, are more often fatal than the ones involving beginners.) At least 85 percent of the accidents occur to climbers without guides. M. Henry concluded that the number of accidents is increasing faster, in proportion, than the number of climbers, which has also been steadily increasing. Some of the increase in the accident rate, he felt, was due, ironically, to an increase in the excellence of the mountain rescue services, which has given some climbers the attitude of, in his words, "*Après tout, on viendra me chercher, et cela ne coûtera rien*" ("After all, they'll come and find me, and it won't cost me anything"). There have been some spectacular recent applications of this attitude.

In September, 1965, the alpine community was stunned by an accident that took the lives of two of the best climbers in Europe—Marc Martinetti, a young Chamonix guide, and Lionel Terray, also a Chamonix guide, whom many people regarded as the greatest expeditionary climber who ever lived. No one will ever know exactly how they were killed. Together, they had been climbing a difficult *falaise* near Grenoble, and, having negotiated the hardest part of it, they fell while doing a relatively easy passage near the summit. (When a great climber does have an accident, it not uncom-

* By comparison, in 1987 there were forty-one fatal mountaineering accidents in the United States and Canada, a fairly typical number.

145

monly occurs while he is moving very quickly on easy terrain.) I did not know Martinetti, who was twenty-five when he died, but I had come to know Terray and his family through Jaccoux, who lived for a while in a small chalet on the Terray property in Chamonix. Terray was one of the most remarkable men I have ever met. He gave the impression of invulnerable physical strength combined with a lucid intelligence and great warmth of personality. His physical courage was legendary. During the first successful assault on Annapurna, in the Himalayas, in 1950, it was Terray who, at the risk of losing his own fingers—and thus his livelihood as a guide—undoubtedly saved the lives of his companions by massaging their limbs and giving them his gloves. Physically, he was not especially well built for climbing. He was heavy, and his arms were rather short. But at forty-four—his age when he died—he told me that he still constantly did gymnastics to improve his agility—something unheard of for a guide, who keeps fit simply by doing his job. Terray's alpine experiences, wonderfully described in his book *Les Conquérants de l'Inutile,* so often balanced him on the thinnest margin between life and death that for alpinists he became a symbol, as Jaccoux put it in a letter to me, "of the myth of invulnerability, of good fortune, of the great climber who would never be killed in the mountains."

Terray was what French climbers call *"un pur."* He simply and plainly loved the mountains, and his exploits came as a consequence of his love, and not of any desire for personal publicity or acclaim. He belonged to an old tradition of idealistic mountaineers—a tradition that, like so many traditions, is in danger of disappearing because of the temptations offered by the mass publicity media. To Americans it may seem curious that there could *be* any temptations that radio, newspapers, magazines, and television might offer an alpinist. In our country, the mountains, for most people, are far away, and what happens in them is of relatively little interest. However, in Europe tens of thousands, if not hundreds of thousands, of people climb, hike, and ski. And the number is increasing all the time. The great alpine communities like Chamonix, Zermatt, Kitzbühel, and Cortina are familiar to most Europeans, and in a place like Chamonix, where the most spectacular climbs are made and the most tragic accidents occur, many French newspapers keep "stringers"; the magazine *Paris-Match* had a full-time correspondent on hand there all summer, just in case something happened. Indeed, it has now become fashionable for European newspapers to sponsor sensational climbs. In return for financial support, a climber will sell the rights to his story and his photographs, and the editors no doubt hope that something out of the ordinary will occur. After Terray's death, the next stunning alpine accident developed out of just such a newspaper-sponsored climb. It came about on the North Wall of the Eiger.

The Eigerwand—the Eiger's North Wall—is regarded as the most dangerous of the great alpine climbs. Most of the approaches to the summit of the Eiger are over relatively easy glacial terrain, but the North Wall, which looms more than six thousand feet above the tiny village of Kleine Scheidegg, in the Bernese Oberland of Switzerland, is a fantastic, vertiginous maze of rock, snow, and ice. The Swiss, with their instinct for tourism, have constructed a cog railroad that passes *inside* the Eiger and ultimately deposits the passenger in the magnificent alpine setting of the Jungfraujoch. En route, the train occasionally stops at what is called the Eiger Station, where the passenger can get out and walk down a rather frigid illuminated tunnel to a window that has been cut in the North Wall. The window is about a third of the way up the wall, and the sight that greets the viewer is not exactly calculated to encourage him to start a career of alpinism. He is perched over a vertical expanse of rock and ice, down which flow constant streams of water, snow, and stones; these avalanches constitute one of the more dubious charms of venturing out onto the wall.

The North Wall has had a turbulent history. In 1936, after several fatal accidents—especially to German climbers, who were hoping to dedicate a victory over the wall to Hitler— the Canton of Bern made an attempt to prohibit climbing on it. One wonders how this ban was supposed to be enforced, and, indeed, it was lifted shortly thereafter. In late August, 1938, a mixed German and Austrian party made the first ascent. It was not until 1947 that the second ascent was made—by Terray and the great French climber Louis Lachenal. By March, 1966, the wall had been climbed by fifty-five different parties (about 150 people in all), and there had been twenty-six deaths. In that year, it occurred to several climbers—among them an American, John Harlin—that the Eiger's North Wall was ripe for a *"direttissima."* A *"direttissima"* (the "super-direct") has been defined as the route that a drop of water would take if it were to fall from the top of a peak to the bottom. There are no first ascents of particular peaks left in the Alps, so climbers who are interested in making a reputation specialize in pioneering difficult routes on peaks that have been climbed. The ultimate in such route-pioneering is the *direttissima.*

Harlin, who fell to his death in March, 1966, during the *direttissima* on the Eiger, was, like Terray, a remarkable physical specimen. Before taking up climbing, he had been an Air Force jet pilot. He had also studied costume designing. He once told me he had done a good deal of motorcycle racing in California, but James Ramsey Ullman, in a biography of Harlin, *Straight Up,* observed that he was not above embellishing his own myth when it suited him; since there is no mention of motorcycle racing in the book, this may have been an example. According to Mr. Ullman, Harlin had in his character a streak of violence, and, indeed, often claimed that he had killed a man in a street fight. He was married, and he and his wife taught school during the winter in the Swiss community of Leysin. Like Terray, he had had innumerable escapes in the mountains. He was thirty-one when he died. His expedition up the Eiger was sponsored by the English newspaper the *Telegraph,* which paid the cost of the equipment and also of an airplane that Harlin rented to survey the face, so that he could trace out his route. Harlin conceived of the attack as a kind of miniature Himalayan expedition. He planned to establish "camps"—really caves dug in the snow—at various places on the wall, and had decided to try the *direttissima* in the winter, since he hoped that the rockfall might be at a minimum then. When he and his group arrived at Kleine Scheidegg, they found an even larger German party, subsidized by a German publisher and accompanied by its own public-relations director, also ready to attempt the *direttissima.* Although the press built up the climb as a race for the summit, the two parties ultimately cooperated. To provision the camps, they fixed ropes on the face of the cliff and used them both for descending from the camps and for climbing back up to them. One climbs such ropes by attaching metal clamps—*jumars*—to them, which, in conjunction with a system of attachable stirrups, enable the climber to go up with relative ease. The major disadvantage of the system is that the *jumars* can abrade the ropes. That is what happened to Harlin; an abraded rope gave way under his weight, and he fell.

The deaths of Terray and Harlin, occurring as they did within a few months of each other, set the scene for the extraordinary events of the coming summer—a series of events that caused many people to wonder whether some sort of regulation should not be introduced into alpine climbing, on the order of the system in the Soviet Union. There a climber must have what amounts to a license, beginning with a "learner's permit" and gradually working up to more and more difficult climbs. Such a system unquestionably prevents many accidents, yet it also—at least, so it is argued—destroys the freedom of expression that is so important a part of mountaineering. The summer following Harlin's death offered some of the worst weather in recent European history. A few days of intermittent sunshine would be followed by a week of extremely bad weather— torrential rain in the valleys and violent snowstorms in the mountains. Mountain weather is almost impossible to predict from day to day under the best of circumstances. In those days, there were two barometers in front of the Guide Bureau in Chamonix. One was a modern, shining metallic apparatus, which, along with the atmospheric pressure, indicated by a red or a green light whether the pressure was rising or falling. It had several other dials, whose precise significance I was never able to penetrate, but I think they measured the density of water vapor, or something. The second barometer was an ancient affair in a wooden case, and it must have dated back many decades. It gave only the barometric pressure, which was marked by an inked needle on a moving paper tape. The needle traced out a curve, so that one could compare readings at different times of the day. A careful observer could note some curious kinks in this curve, which could be ascribed to a habit among the Chamonix guides of giving the instrument a kick when they were unhappy over the barometric situation. I once discussed these barometers with the *doyen* of the Chamonix guides, Armand Couttet, who was then eighty-two and in splendid shape. Our talk was prompted by the fact that Chamonix had just undergone a period of fifteen days of constant rain during which the barometers had announced everything from *"Grand Beau"* to *"Variable."* When I asked him how he felt about the matter, he said, *"On n'a plus confiance dans ces choses-là depuis très longtemps."* Now Chamonix has a weather bureau with a full-fledged meteorologist in the same building that houses the Guide Bureau. It functions during the climbing season, issuing bulletins a few times a day, and these appear to be uncannily accurate. But for an alpinist engaged in a difficult climb, an hour or two of good weather can mean the difference between life and death, and no meteorologist, however competent, can predict the tremendously rapid changes of mountain weather to such a refined degree. Unfortunately, the meteorologist was not in residence in 1966, and climbers had to rely on the two unattended barometers (which are still there, and still being kicked, by the way).

The conclusion that one might draw from all this is that it is foolish to attempt a difficult climb unless the weather conditions appear to be nearly perfect. To understand the events of that summer of 1966, then, one must realize something of the psychology of the alpinist. Most climbers are young and do not have much money. Typically, they are students who have skimped for a whole winter in order to save enough money to come to the Alps for a brief season of climbing—a season that, at best, lasts only six or eight weeks, since in June there is still too much snow for high climbing, and by the first week of September the days are getting too short. Many of the young climbers hitchhike to Chamonix or come on motor scooters, and, to save money, they pitch tents on one or another of the camping grounds nearby. For a climber, there is nothing drearier than sitting in a small tent, with the mountains all around, waiting until the weather clears. On top of this, a young climber who wants to make a reputation is under heavy pressure to do something of great difficulty. (The guides have already earned their reputations, and they can fill in the days of poor weather by taking clients of modest abilities on the numerous classic routes around the valley, from which there are easy retreats if the weather turns really bad.) In addition, a young climber has before him the countless examples of those who have done difficult climbs even in bad weather. Finally, as M. Henry noted in his report on alpine accidents, there is also in the back of the young climber's mind an awareness of the efficient rescue service in the valley—the realization that, if the worst comes to the worst, *"on vous cherche."*

Early in the first week in August, having learned from the Geneva-airport weather service that a temporary spell of clear weather could be expected, three extremely strong French alpinists, including a first-rate guide who had come along for the fun of it, decided to attempt one of the great routes on the Italian side of Mont Blanc. From France, the flanks of Mont Blanc give the impression of a serene glacial slope, and, indeed, anyone with a modicum of experience and a fair amount of training can, with a guide, make the long trudge up with no great difficulty. The summit of Mont Blanc is so large that in bad weather it is quite easy to lose oneself on it, and for this reason alone it is important to be with someone who can find his way down under any circumstances. The Italian side is another matter altogether. From the Valley of Aosta, Mont Blanc is a giant Himalayan wall. There are several routes up the face—routes that have been given rather stirring names, like La Sentinelle Rouge, La Voie Major, and L'Innominata. Apart from the technical difficulties of these routes—which are extreme—the climber must be prepared to cope with arctic cold, winds of over a hundred miles an hour, and the physiological discomforts of the lack of oxygen. In addition, on many of these routes there is literally a point of no return in bad weather.

The lower parts of the climbs involve picking one's way through vast fields of crevasses, and if the visibility is not perfect there is no hope of finding one's way back down. There is an axiom that above a certain point on the Italian routes the only way to safety is over the top and down the easy side. One cannot turn back.

The three alpinists had decided to do La Major, and they were confident that they could do it in twenty-four hours— the time during which the weather was expected to hold stable. The first stop on their route was the refuge-bivouac of La Fourche. I have never been to La Fourche, but I am told that it requires first-class alpinism to get even that far. The three men had installed themselves as comfortably as possible in a tiny, cold bivouac when, to their astonishment, they observed four other climbers, who did not seem to be very strong, making their way toward them. These turned out to be four young French climbers, who announced that they, too, were going to do La Major, even though they did not appear to have either the equipment or the training for such a difficult route. At this point, the guide with the first group told the newcomers, bluntly and plainly, to go back down. (One *can* get back down from La Fourche.) Once a guide agrees to go with a group of climbers, he is not only morally but legally responsible for their safety. In this case, however, the guide, not having been hired by the newcomers, was not in a position to *force* them to return. Something of a quarrel developed, and the first group decided that in order to establish their independence and absolve the guide of any responsibility for the second party, they would move on as soon as possible to the next bivouac. The following morning, when the three men started up, they quickly noticed, to their consternation, that the four others were following them, making use of the trail that the three men had cut in the snow. After a short time, a violent snowstorm suddenly hit

Mont Blanc. (Another of the features of climbing the Italian side is that it is difficult to see the approach of bad weather if it comes, as it often does, over the top from France.) The three men decided that the best thing to do was to establish an emergency bivouac in the shelter of a shallow crevasse and to go on to the summit if the weather showed any sign of clearing. Shortly, they were joined by the four others, and the seven men spent the next forty-eight hours huddled shoulder to shoulder in the subzero temperatures of the crevasse. At the end of the forty-eight hours, there was still no sign of clearing, and the guide decided that now they *must* get to the top if they were not to die of exposure. They started up, and within twenty meters one of the young French climbers fell exhausted to the snow. Under any less desperate conditions, it might have been possible for the rest of the group to carry him, but in the near hundred-mile-an-hour winds, the freezing cold, and the heavy snow there was nothing to be done. At this point, his companion on the rope—the four young Frenchmen had been roped together in pairs—heroically decided that he would stay with his fallen comrade. After leaving the two of them with as much clothing and food as they could spare, the five remaining men pushed on to the summit. There another of the young French climbers passed out from exhaustion, and his rope-mate, too, elected to stay with him. The three original climbers proceeded down the French side as fast as they could to get help, and, in the worst weather conditions imaginable, the mountain rescue service of the French police succeeded in flying a helicopter to the summit of Mont Blanc. There the crew found the two young climbers still alive but at the limit of their strength; below the summit, they found the two other climbers together, frozen to death. *On vous cherche.*

Within ten days of this tragedy, there occurred in Chamonix what was without doubt the most complicated and dramatic mountain rescue in the history of the Alps. By the time it was over, it had required the services of forty-four French alpine troops, six mountain policemen, eight Chamonix guides, and ten voluntary alpinists. It involved seventy helicopter flights and nearly a mile of climbing rope, all of it left behind. The cost of the undertaking was more than $10,000 and the life of one of the rescuers, a German climber who had volunteered his services. *On vous cherche.* In addition, the rescue operation brought to light one of the most remarkable personalities in contemporary alpinism—Gary (Gareth) Hemming, an American whom the European newspapers soon christened "the beatnik of the Alps" and who came to symbolize the drama and heroism of the rescue. In addition to everything else, Hemming proved to have an odd sense of mischief, and it was not easy, as countless interviewers found out after the rescue, to get clearcut answers from him about his life and career. He was extremely tall—perhaps six feet six. (After the rescue, he told a journalist, with great solemnity, that he was originally only six feet four but that during the war in the Pacific he had been captured by the Japanese, who had stretched him. When the journalist dutifully took this down in his notes, Hemming said that he was only kidding—the truth was that he was six feet six at birth.) Piecing together various accounts, and making a generous allowance for Bunyanesque hyperbole, one would hazard that Hemming was born in Pasadena, California, around 1933, and that he studied for a while at San Diego State College but, finding the regimentation intolerable, came to France. From what I have been able to make out, he studied philosophy for a while at the University of Grenoble, and afterward lived, one way or another, on the five dollars a week that his mother sent him. Needless to say, this regime imposed certain economies; in fact, during several winters Hemming resided under various bridges over the Seine, depending to some extent on mountaineering friends in Paris for more substantial lodging and sustenance when these were available. In the summers, he usually resided in a small tent near Chamonix. Hemming's face was absolutely remarkable. It had something of the beauty of the paintings of the Christian saints, and it was crowned with an incredible foliage of long dark-blond hair, so thick that it must have afforded not only considerable thermal insulation but also substantial protection from falling rock. In the mountains, he wore a thick red pullover and one or more pairs of ancient pants, whose multicolored patches gave something of the effect of Joseph's coat. He had a delightful smile, an air of inner strength, and great serenity.

The adventure of which Hemming became the hero began on Sunday, August 14. That day, two German climbers, Heinz Ramisch and Hermann Schridde, began the extremely difficult climb of the West Face of the Dru. The Dru—really Les Drus, since there are twin summits—is one of the most beautiful and impressive mountains in Europe. It towers over the Mer de Glace glacier, above Chamonix, like a needle reaching into the sky. It is unlikely that any climbing routes in the world offer more sustained difficulties than the ones on the faces of the Dru, and it is the ambition of every great climber to tackle them. There is no easy route. The *voie normale*, or standard route, which was fashionable with expert climbers before the war, is technically not of great difficulty, but it is very long and is constantly exposed to falling rock. It is now used mainly as a route of descent by climbers who have taken the extraordinarily difficult routes on the West and North Faces. The West Face of the Dru was first climbed in 1952 by four Frenchmen, and since then the climb has been repeated a few times each year. On that

August Sunday, after being informed that the weather could be expected to hold stable for at least forty-eight hours, Ramisch, a twenty-two-year-old student from Karlsruhe, and Schridde, a thirty-year-old mechanic from Hannover, who had just met and who had never climbed anything together, set out for the West Face. They made an arrangement with some companions who remained below to signal by waving a red parka if they got into trouble. Since they expected the climb to last at least two days, they took with them an extra supply of food and some bivouac equipment. By Monday noon, they had done two-thirds of the face and were at an altitude of about ten thousand feet. There, they were struck by a violent storm—snow, hail, and lightning. (The Dru, because of its needle shape, is an especially frequent target of lightning.) Their first thought was to get down. They had just surmounted one of the principal obstacles of the route, a *dièdre*—a vertical cleft in the rock made where two faces join each other at an angle—of ninety meters, and they rappelled back down it and bivouacked at its foot, in the hope that the weather would change. At daybreak, they awoke to find the whole lower portion of the mountain covered with sheets of ice. It was at this point that, by their own admission, they made a mistake in judgment that nearly cost them their lives. Instead of continuing down, which would have been feasible, though delicate, they decided to go *up,* and so escape over the top; they felt that the part above, which they could not see, might be clear. So they went back up the *dièdre.* Above the *dièdre,* the route up the West Face takes a curious twist. The face is climbed by a series of more or less parallel vertical fissures. To go from one fissure to the next, it is necessary from time to time to displace oneself *sidewise* along the face. This is done by what is known as a "pendulum rappel." As the name implies, the climber swings from his rope, which is attached to

157

a piton, in a series of arcs until he gets to where he wants to go. Quite clearly, this maneuver can be used only if there is a suitable landing place at the end of the arc. At this point in the route on the West Face, a pendulum rappel was called for. The landing place was a small terrace, about six feet long and three feet wide. The two Germans executed the rappel and then, to their horror, discovered that the rock above the terrace, instead of being dry and climbable, was impassable, because of a thick covering of ice. Moreover, Ramisch had developed a sore throat so painful that he could no longer swallow, and his companion had severely bruised his ribs in a fall while climbing the *dièdre*. The only possible way to get off the terrace was to make an extremely difficult, and very dangerous, traverse across the vertical face to a point where the West Face and the North Face joined, and then to climb down the North Face—which in itself is very difficult. Leading from their terrace the two Germans found some strands of rope attached to pitons that had been put into the rock in 1952, when the original French group climbed the West Face, but since it had been exposed to the weather for fourteen years, the two climbers decided that it was unlikely to support their weight. According to later reports, they disagreed about whether they should try to go on, and in the end they settled down on their terrace, ten thousand feet in the air, and prepared a bivouac, which was to last for the next *seven days*.

It was now Tuesday, August 16. Realizing that they were trapped, the two Germans signaled for help to their companions below. During the summer, mountain rescue in Chamonix is nearly a full-time job, and it is so taxing and dangerous that it used to be split up among three principal groups—the Chamonix guides, who were responsible for all rescues until August 1; the École Nationale de Ski et d'Alpinisme, in Chamonix, which trains all the guides in France and was responsible for rescues during the first two weeks of August; and the École de Haute Montagne, which trains French alpine troops and took over until the first of September, when it was again the turn of the guides. These organizations all worked coöperatively with the Péleton Spécialisé de Haute Montagne, a division of the French police, which, in addition to specially trained personnel, has at its disposal several Alouette III helicopters and a radio station that maintains communications with many of the refuges in the region. This group is now responsible for *all* rescues in Chamonix. Since the accident occurred in the third week of August, under the old system the job of getting the Germans down fell to Colonel André Gonnet, the officer in charge of the alpine troops. From the valley there was no way of knowing whether the Germans were injured, or even—since the weather had by now turned so bad that one could not even see the Dru from Chamonix—whether they were still alive. The first thing to do was to dispatch a helicopter to the Dru to find out what their condition was. (*Paris-Match* later published some remarkable photographs showing the Alouette hovering like a forlorn lost insect a few meters from the terrace where the climbers were trapped.) In good weather, the rescue might have been accomplished by helicopter—or, at least, provisions might have been dropped to the climbers. As it was, the only thing the helicopter crew was able to do was to catch intermittent glimpses of the Germans and so ascertain that they were still alive. Not knowing their physical condition, Colonel Gonnet had to assume the worst. He therefore dispatched a platoon—over forty alpine troops, with their own guides— to the base of the Dru. The idea was to get a strong group of climbers to the summit by the *voie normale* and then drop a steel cable down the face. Rescuers could be lowered to the terrace by the cable, and the two climbers winched up. This plan meant that the troops had to carry very heavy equipment up the *voie normale*, which was covered with snow and ice, and along which there were violent discharges of lightning. (Several of the soldiers received minor electrical burns during this part of the operation.) Moreover, the terrace on which the climbers were trapped was situated under some enormous overhanging rocks—*les grands surplombs*—which meant that any cable lowered down the face would be beyond their reach. On Wednesday and Thursday, Colonel Gonnet proceeded with what the newspapers came to call "the invasion of the Dru." By this time, Chamonix itself had been invaded—by newspapermen from all over Europe, by television crews, and by a team from O.R.T.F., the French national radio-and-television network, who came equipped with their own helicopter. Every newspaper in Western Europe carried details of the rescue operation on its front pages.

At noon on Thursday, August 18, Gary Hemming was sitting in a café in Courmayeur, the delightful alpine town at the Italian end of the tunnel that leads under Mont Blanc. With him was a young German friend, Lothar Mauch, with whom he had driven from Chamonix. They were planning to do a climb together, but Hemming was reading an account of the accident on the Dru in the *Dauphiné Libéré*, a paper published in the French department of the Haute-Savoie. Suddenly he turned to Mauch and said that he had to go back to Chamonix. Among all climbers, Hemming was one of the greatest experts on the West Face of the Dru. He had been on it many times, and had even pioneered a new route; above all, he knew how to get down the face in any kind of weather. He felt that he could not stand by and watch two men gradually die of exposure when he had the technical skill to save their lives. Mauch did not need much persuasion, and soon the two of them were heading back to Chamonix.

At three o'clock that afternoon, Hemming presented himself to Colonel Gonnet. The Colonel apparently had a little difficulty recognizing Hemming, since he had recently shaved off his beard. The beard had become an issue a year or so before, when Hemming was invited to join a specially selected group of alpinists for a training course at the École Nationale. When he showed up, he was told that he would not be admitted to the course unless he got a shave and a haircut, which he refused to do. He was not admitted, but sometime after the course was over he removed his beard anyway. In any case, the Colonel was pleased to accept his offer of help and, in return, supplied Hemming with army equipment, including a light two-way radio and some specially prepared rucksacks containing provisions for the two Germans, if they could be reached in time. Hemming recruited four very strong alpinists in addition to Mauch: another German, named Gehrad; an English specialist on the Dru named Mick Burke, who later died on Mount Everest; and two French climbers. By seven that evening, Hemming and his team were on the cog railroad that winds upward to a point above the Mer de Glace glacier, which must be crossed to reach the foothills that lead to the Dru, and by three the following morning they were on the glacier itself. (Hemming was offered the use of helicopters to transport his group to the base of the Dru, but he was afraid that flying might be delayed by the bad weather, and he knew that the Germans were fighting a losing battle against time.) At ten in the morning, they began the climb up the long and very dangerous Couloir du Dru, a corridor that leads to the West Face and is notorious for rockfall and avalanches. By two in the afternoon, they were on the West Face itself, and it had begun to snow heavily.

Meanwhile, in Chamonix, another bizarre aspect of the story was unfolding. A renowned French climber and Chamonix guide, René Desmaison—also a leading expert on the Dru—had set forth on his own, without making contact with any of the professional rescue groups in the valley, to undertake what amounted to an independent rescue mission up the West Face. Both Hemming and Desmaison had independently reached the conclusion that the only way to save the climbers was to follow the route that the climbers themselves had used, and then bring them down by the same route. One cannot fault Desmaison's skill and courage—nothing is more dangerous than a rescue in bad weather—but he was severely criticized for undertaking such a private operation without consulting the authorities in the valley; indeed, shortly after the rescue the Company of Chamonix Guides voted to exclude him for what was regarded as an intolerable breach of discipline.

Ironically, in February, 1971, Desmaison was himself the subject of a dramatic helicopter rescue. On the tenth of the month, accompanied by a twenty-four-year-old fellow-guide, Serge Gousseault, he set out to establish a new route on the north face of the Grandes Jorasses, near Chamonix—one of the most difficult climbing faces in all the Alps. The winter had been marked by rather little snowfall, and the conditions were especially favorable for winter climbing, with long periods of rather mild, stable weather. As luck would have it, by the thirteenth, the pair, now halfway up the face, were caught in a severe snowstorm, which slowed them down and which was followed by a second storm on the fifteenth. By the sixteenth, Gousseault's hands were so severely frostbitten that he could no longer use them, and Desmaison was literally dragging him up the mountain, rope length after rope length. The pair still had radio communication with Desmaison's wife, in the valley, and as late as the sixteenth Desmaison gave no indication that anything was wrong. On the night of the seventeenth, there was a third storm, and by the nineteenth, although the two men were nearly at the summit, Gousseault could not continue farther. By this time, a helicopter had been dispatched from Chamonix to investigate, and although the pilot succeeded in flying close to the pair, he did not get any signal from Desmaison that he could interpret as an S.O.S. (In the subsequent inquiry, there was a difference of opinion between Desmaison and the pilot as to what signals had, in fact, been given.) In any case, despite a brief spell of very good weather on the twentieth, no rescue attempt was called for, and on the night of the twenty-first Gousseault died of exposure. By this time, Desmaison was so exhausted that he could not get to the summit alone. Bad weather set in again, and no helicopter could set down near the summit until the morning of the twenty-fifth. Then a rescue team was lowered from the summit by cable, and in less than three hours Desmaison was brought up and transported to the hospital in Chamonix. As a commentator in the February, 1971, issue of *La Montagne* noted, "It was just in time. He would not have survived another night." The commentator went on, "Once more, René Desmaison has exhibited his exceptional physical resistance and his courage in adversity. But many alpinists wonder about his choice of a companion for such an enterprise in such a season [Gousseault had never done any serious winter climbing], and about his decision to continue despite the fact that the conditions had become unfavorable." The commentator also went on to criticize the various newspapers and magazines that had treated the whole matter as if it somehow merited respect: *"On eût souhaité plus de pudeur,"* he wrote. He concluded, "These dramatic events in the Jorasses should be carefully studied both by individual Alpinists and by the mountain rescue organizations; there are many lessons to be learned on each side." *On vous cherche.*

Whatever Desmaison's motives may have been in undertaking to rescue the two Germans, there was no doubt but
that the journalists and television people exerted all sorts of
persuasion, monetary and otherwise, on the principals in
the rescue in order to obtain exclusive reports and pictures.
Recently, Lothar Mauch (who now owns a very successful
chain of Mod boutiques—Lothar's—in France) told me that
a representative of an important magazine had at one point
physically tried to shove a camera and some film into the
hands of the Hemming people as they were leaving for the
Mer de Glace. Mauch said that they finally told the man that
they would smash his camera if he did not take it back. Like
all alpinists, Hemming had a small camera with him, but he
and Mauch agreed that if they did not find the climbers alive
and safe they would destroy the film without showing it to
anyone.

In any case, at five o'clock on the afternoon of Friday,
August 19, Hemming, camped on the West Face, observed
Desmaison and a companion, Vincent Mercié, moving up
the face somewhat below. Hemming immediately decided to
join forces, and when Desmaison arrived the next morning
the group split into two units of four, with the strongest
climbers going ahead and the others following to equip the
face with fixed ropes as a line of retreat. That night, the eight
men bivouacked together on the wall. Originally, Hemming
had thought that he might be able to reach the Germans in a
day, but, as he later admitted, he had not even imagined the
severity of conditions on the Dru. At noon on Saturday,
nobody knew when—or even whether—the Germans could
be reached from the West Face. Consequently, the École
Nationale and the Guide Bureau decided that they would
send a group of guides, chosen from the best and most rapid
climbers available, up the North Face, with the idea of reaching the Germans from slightly above their terrace. The army

was still engaged in its steel-cable operation at the summit, and among the dangers that beset the climbers on both faces was the fall of blocks of ice unavoidably kicked loose by the soldiers as they installed their heavy equipment. It was during one of these maneuvers that the German climber Wolfgang Egle, who was a friend of the trapped men, and who had volunteered to help, lost his life. As nearly as one can tell, while doing a rappel from the top, he somehow became snarled in one of his ropes and was strangled.

By 6:00 A.M. on Sunday, August 21, Hemming was close enough to the Germans to talk to them. "We are coming," is what he said, and by noon he and Desmaison were there. For six days, the Germans had been living on a tiny ration of nuts, one of the last of which they peeled and offered to Hemming, who remarked to Desmaison that if the stranded men had been French they would have eaten everything the first day. About five minutes later, the head of one of the Chamonix guides who had been going up the North Wall appeared just above the terrace. A discussion ensued as to the safest way to get everyone back down; the guides on the North Wall favored lowering a rope to the terrace and maneuvering the two exhausted Germans onto their wall, which they had equipped for the descent. Hemming said that he would feel more comfortable taking the men down the route *he* had come up. Since he had reached the trapped men first, it was decided that it was up to him to bring them down as he saw fit. After giving the Germans some solid food and warm clothing, the entire group began the hazardous descent of the West Face. It was not until Monday, after still another bivouac on the Dru, that the party reached the safety of the glacier below. The following morning—when, as one of the newspaper reporters somewhat cynically observed, the light was bright enough so that the

O.R.T.F. television cameras could obtain excellent pictures—the two Germans and their rescuers were transported to Chamonix by helicopter.

Ramisch, the younger of the two men, appeared to be almost untouched by the effects of spending nine days on the Dru, and Schridde, in the hospital in Chamonix, soon recovered from his rib injury and exposure. In one of the interviews Ramisch gave, he said that the only thing he regretted about the whole adventure was the loss of his friend Egle. (In the October, 1967, issue of *La Montagne*, there was a brief postscript on the accident published in "La Chronique Alpine"—a periodic summary of alpine events. The "Chronique" noted that in August, 1967, a well-known French guide, Yannick Seigneur, and a client found themselves in a storm on exactly the same ledge as the Germans. They were, however, able to make—unaided—the traverse to the North Face, which they said was not especially difficult except perhaps psychologically, since the passage takes place over *"le vide impressionnant."* The note concluded, "This illustrates the incompetence of the German climbers, who did absolutely nothing to get out of the dangerous predicament they found themselves in.")

In 1971, Desmaison, who still has a large and active climbing clientele, published his autobiography, *La Montagne à Mains Nues*. In it, he writes of the events on the Dru as he views them. He is, as one might imagine, rather bitter about his expulsion from the Company of Chamonix Guides. He writes, "One heard certain writers who took themselves to be guides, or certain guides who took themselves to be writers, making pompous declarations when they probably had never once taken part in any rescue worthy of the name. *L'occasion était vraiment trop belle."* He adds, "Helping someone in danger is not only a duty but an obligation. For a guide, it is a question of honor. . . . If the

The end of a successful alpine rescue. Gary Hemming is at the right of the photograph, wearing a long scarf and cap; René Desmaison is above and to the left of Hemming, and just to the left of Desmaison are the two rescued German climbers, Hermann Schridde and Heinz Ramisch. Lothar Mauch is at the far left of the photograph, with his leg stretched forward. (*Paris-Match*)

same situation were to arise again, and if my intervention would be helpful, *eh bien, ce que j'ai fait je le recommencerais.*"

As for Hemming, he suddenly became an internationally acclaimed hero. Some time after the rescue Jaccoux and I were riding the 6:15 A.M. *téléphérique* up into the Aiguilles of Chamonix, and there in the car was Hemming, in his red sweater and his ancient pair of mountain pants. He and Jaccoux were close friends. "*Où tu vas?*" asked Jaccoux. "For a little walk," Hemming answered, with a mischievous smile. Later, Jaccoux told me that Hemming never informed anyone where he was going, so that "a little walk" really could have been a little walk or, as had been the case earlier that summer, an attempt to make a very difficult first ascent. I had heard that Hemming was writing a book, so I asked him how it was coming along. "Oh, the book," he said vaguely. "The book is something I tell people about who ask me what I do. It's curious that people who ask you that sort of question seem to be particularly pleased if you tell them that you're writing a book." The *téléphérique* came to a stop, and we all got off, Jaccoux and I to proceed on foot, and Hemming to take the connecting *téléphérique "vers le haut."* When he left us, he said softly, perhaps as much to himself as to us, using one of the kindest farewells that climbers exchange before going into the mountains, "*Allez, et bonne course.*"

On August 6, 1969, Hemming was found shot to death in Grand Teton Park, in Wyoming. It is presumed that he had committed suicide. He had spent the preceding winter in Chamonix working at removing the snow from the roofs of the taller buildings in the valley. In the spring, he set off to hitchhike to Alaska, where he planned to work in the forests. Many of his friends in Chamonix received postcards from him from Alaska—postcards full of his usual irreverence and gaiety. After his death, some of his closest friends said that Hemming had often talked of a day when he might lose his love for the mountains and his love for life. Why such a day should have come among the great mountains of Wyoming no one will ever really know.

6

Une Bonne Ballade

On July 19, 1965, the tunnel under Mont Blanc between Chamonix, in France, and Courmayeur, in Italy, was opened to the public a few days after General de Gaulle, who had come to Chamonix for *la grande ouverture*, figured in a splendid ceremony culminating in a trip through the tunnel with the president of Italy. I myself traveled through the tunnel a few weeks later. It is a slick affair—two comfortable lanes, air-conditioned all the way, with flashing lights that tell you that you are going too fast or too slow, or are too close to the car in front of you. In ten minutes you are in Italy. The tunnel is good for the tourist trade and it dramatically shortens the time it takes a businessman to drive from Geneva to Rome. And it represents the end of an era.

Before the tunnel, the only way to go directly from Chamonix to Italy was by crossing a high mountain pass. To be sure, in recent years one could make the trip over the glaciers by *téléphérique*, but until then the only way to go was on foot. Alpine literature is full of accounts of crisscrossings of these passes. Ever since I began mountain climbing in and around the Chamonix Valley, I have been reading chronicles of the early climbs and pass crossings, and it occurred to me that just before the tunnel opened might be a good time to make a complete circuit of Mont Blanc by means of the glacial passes and valleys that surround it. The trip takes about five days, winding its way through seven valleys in three countries, and it would be a kind of tribute to the pioneers as well as a chance to see some completely new landscape.

As soon as I got to Geneva, where I was going to be working during the summer, I phoned Jaccoux, and asked him whether he would be interested in making such a trip. He was delighted with the idea and said, to my surprise, that although he had been climbing around Chamonix for nearly fifteen years, he had never done *le tour de Mont Blanc*. He also said that if he could garage his then six-year-old daughter with her grandparents, he was sure that his wife Michèle, a former Olympic skier and now a ski instructor, would be glad to come along, too. A few days later, he phoned back to say that Michèle could come, and we fixed the first of July as the date on which to begin the trip. Shortly after *that*, I found myself in La Hutte, a sports shop in Chamonix, buying all sorts of equipment.

To get some idea of what we had in mind, and to see why the equipment was necessary, it is helpful to review a little of the geography of the Mont Blanc region. The Mont Blanc massif itself is a high glacial plateau about thirty miles long and ten miles wide. It runs from the southwest to the north-east, starting in France and ending in Switzerland, and the Franco-Italian border is traced along most of its length. It is ringed by a system of seven valleys—a giant ice castle surrounded by a moat. The classic tour of the massif involves following a well-marked trail through the valleys, and it would be nothing if it were not that at several points on the circuit the headwall that separates one valley from the next blocks the track. Many of these headwalls, reaching out radially, like the spokes of a wheel, are more than ten thousand feet high and are covered with snow all year long. Still, to traverse them requires no alpinism; the trip is simply a good hard walk. There are elaborate alpine refuges spaced at a comfortable day's march apart, and the whole thing takes about a week. That, at least, is the usual routine; we wanted to do something different. We wanted to make the circuit while staying as high on the shoulder of the massif as possible. This meant that we would be moving almost all the time among the glaciers that tumble down the sides of Mont Blanc. On the Italian sector, however, where the valley walls are impossibly steep, we would join the usual trail until we reached Switzerland, and then move back up on the glaciers. Our trip, like all glacier traveling, *would* involve some alpinism, and Jaccoux thought that we might bag en route a few of the peaks that border some of the high passes we expected to cross. He was not sure of the exact course we would follow, and while I was buying the equipment he talked it over with Roger Frison-Roche, the guide and mountain writer whose book, *Mont Blanc and the Seven Valleys*, had given me the idea for the expedition in the first place.

There had been an especially heavy snowfall the previous winter, and since we were making our tour early in the season, before the snow had had much chance to melt, we expected that the conditions would be rather wintry. In addition, we were not sure that the refuges would be open, and

Le tour de Mont Blanc

to be on the safe side we planned to carry enough food so that if we arrived at a closed refuge (even if the refuges are officially closed, a door or window is usually left open, so that people can use them unofficially if they have to), we would not go hungry. Jaccoux reasoned that if worse came to worst, we would be able to drop down to one of the tiny villages in the valleys below and find shelter. I made sure that I had at least two of everything—two pairs of gloves, two sweaters, two sets of *stop-tout* (cloth puttees that fit over the tops of one's climbing boots to keep out the snow)—and a new pair of boots. Buying a pair of climbing boots at the beginning of the season is a ceremonial occasion. New boots are things of beauty, wonderfully made out of thick leather and carefully lined with a spongy material to make walking as comfortable as possible. As I was trying on something like the fifth pair and answering innumerable questions about our plans asked by various guides and climbers who had wandered into La Hutte and whose curiosity was aroused by where I might be going with so much equipment so early in the season, Jaccoux appeared, full of optimism about the trip after his talk with Frison-Roche. He suggested that I buy a pair of boots named after a well-known Swiss guide, Michel Darbellay, and this turned out to be a prophetic choice, since we ran into Darbellay himself, in one of the Swiss valleys along our route. Everyone told us that we were going to enjoy *"une bonne ballade,"* and that we would come back bronzed and fit. I don't regret the trip for a second, but, as it turned out, it was not what I would call a *ballade.*

After collecting our gear, Jaccoux and I drove to the small farmhouse where he and Michèle were living. We had lunch with Claude's father, who had come to pick up his granddaughter, and were soon driving down the Chamonix Valley. We were going to start our circuit from the village of Les Contamines in the adjoining Vallée de Montjoie. The pioneers, no doubt, would have done this lap of the trip on foot, but there is a superhighway that leads out of the Chamonix Valley, and it seemed rather silly not to take advantage of it. Our first stop was to be a refuge on the edge of the Glacier de Trélatête—a walk of a few hours from Les Contamines. We planned to cross over the glaciers at the southwestern end of the massif, crossing the Italian border at the same time; it was a shortcut that would save us a two-day march around the end of the massif. On the way to Les Contamines, Jaccoux had the happy notion of stopping at the home of the guardian of the refuge to see if he was at his post. The guardian answered the door himself and told Jaccoux that the refuge was untended, adding that he had left a window open and that we should have no trouble finding it and climbing through. It was fortunate that we had stopped. In Chamonix we had been told that the refuge, which operates as a small hotel during the season, would almost certainly be open; now we added some extra food for that evening's dinner and for breakfast the next morning.

We left the car at the highest point we could drive it to and began the long climb up the slopes to the refuge. Early along, we passed a sign saying that it would take an hour and a half to get there. Jaccoux moves very quickly in the mountains, and Michèle, who was in superb condition after a winter of daily skiing, walks as fast as he does. They soon left me behind. My only previous outing that season had been a brief climb the week before with Jaccoux in the Vercors, near Grenoble. We had done Mont Aiguille—a remarkable tower, about seven thousand feet high, that was known in the Middle Ages as one of "the Seven Miracles of the Dauphiny." All its walls are perfectly vertical, while the top is a level pasture large enough to graze cattle—if one could get them up there. Only one route to the summit can be negotiated without the most advanced techniques, and this route, which involves some middling rock climbing, was done on June 28, 1492, by one Antoine de Ville, lord of Domjulien and of Beaupré. According to a contemporary account, de Ville made use of ladders and "sobtilz engins"— no one seems to know what these were—and he camped on the top for three days in a hut he built. The climbing of Mont Aiguille is the first recorded instance of a serious rock climb, and it is one of the remarkable incidents in the history of alpinism.

As we moved up the trail, clouds began to form, and it was clear that we were in for a storm. Before long, lightning began playing over the ridges above me, and every once in a while I could make out Claude and Michèle along the trail in the distance. It was a good two and a half hours before we reached the refuge. (Jaccoux figured that the time on the sign had probably been deliberately shortened to lure tourists to the refuge, which is privately owned.) By now, it was raining solidly, and we were making our way by flashlight. The refuge consists of two stone buildings, and in the smaller of the two we found the unlocked window. Jaccoux climbed in, then Michèle. I handed our packs in through the window and went to a nearby trough to fill our canteens with icy water. By the time I climbed through the window, Michèle had already begun to straighten up the barnlike room that we found ourselves in. There were long wooden decks on which straw mattresses could be placed for sleeping, and we found a vast number of dusty mattresses and comfortable-looking blankets stacked in every corner of the room. Each of us fixed up a bed, and then Michèle got dinner, Jaccoux studied our maps, and I rested. After dinner, a tremendous electrical storm broke over the refuge, and we turned in for the night to the accompaniment of the rolling echoes of thunder.

After what seemed like a very short time, I heard Jaccoux

calling, *"Debout, mes pauvres! On y va!"* I struggled up from my nest of blankets and, looking sleepily out the window, saw that the sky was thickly overcast. It was not actually raining, but the air had the heavy smell of ozone produced by the lightning of the previous night. We had breakfast, straightened up the room, packed our gear, and climbed back out the window. A narrow, stony trail led onto the glacier. When we reached the ice and snow, at perhaps six in the morning, Jaccoux stopped, took out a climbing rope, and tied Michèle in the middle of it and me on the end. In the gray half-light, the glacier, about five miles long, was not a very appealing sight, and I felt some sympathy with a noted French alpinist who wrote, "Then, at the very first peep of dawn, I discovered the glacier of Trélatête. Through all the Alps I know of no more solitary or more forbidding glacier. And that was what I felt when I saw it in the wan light of early morning. It did not resemble at all what I expected. It looked like a gigantic dead beast—some dragon drowned forever between desolate banks. The whole landscape was deeply inhuman and hostile, as if distorted by the light dripping from the dull sky. It was cold, and the cold permeated my whole being, gripping my heart and numbing my body. I felt terribly lost, miserable, a prey to blind but prodigious powers. And I felt terrified." Claude and Michèle and I were cold, all right, but the slope was gentle and the crevasses easily crossed, so we moved steadily ahead. On all sides, we could see the murky outlines of the great mountains, their summits covered with clouds. We were in a narrow glacial valley, and the sides looked so steep that I did not see how we could possibly get out, but after an hour or so, Jaccoux began navigating toward a steep snow slope leading to the Mont Tondu col, or pass, and by kicking out steps in the hard snow we got up to a rock outcropping that overlooked the glacier. Jaccoux sat down heavily, and I asked him whether he had stopped to take pictures or something, since he normally stops only to keep his clients from collapsing. *"Je m'arrête pour m'arrêter,"* he responded dourly. The heavy atmosphere had made hard work of walking and climbing, and I was pleased to see that I was not the only one to get tired. Jaccoux decided that we would move more easily if we put on our crampons and this we did. It was now beginning to snow lightly, and by the time we reached the top of the pass we were being doused by a mixture of snow and rain.

The sight that greeted us there was as desolate as anything one could imagine. To our right there was a long, dark rock ridge that led up to the summit of Mont Tondu (ten thousand feet), and every few minutes the whole ridge appeared to shake when it got hit by lightning. (Later, when we finally returned to Chamonix, I was gratified to read in Edward Whymper's great alpine classic, *Scrambles Amongst the Alps*, that he had crossed the Col du Mont Tondu 101 years before us, almost to the day, and also in a severe lightning storm.) Ahead of us, across several snow slopes broken up by long rock ridges, we could make out another col—the Col de la Seigne, which marked the Italian frontier. But to move on from the crest of our pass involved dropping down a steep rock wall. It would not have been particularly difficult under normal conditions, but now the rock was slippery and wet and covered with new snow. I inched my way down as far as the rope would let me, while Claude and Michèle anchored me from above. Then I pulled the rope in taut while we got Michèle down, and we both gave Jaccoux whatever security we could while he came down to join us. Finally, I was able to jump out onto the snow, and soon we were together on what appeared to be easy terrain. The only trouble was that the snow was soft, and every few steps one of us would fall through the crust up to the waist. Since there was no real danger, Claude unroped us so we could move somewhat faster. The Jaccoux began to ski down the slopes on their feet, using their ice axes as brakes whenever necessary. I tried to imitate them, but on the first attempt I slipped and began sailing down the long slope on my back, experiencing a sort of sense of suspended animation while the terrain floated past. After sliding for a hundred feet or so, I managed to roll over on my stomach, dig my ice axe into the snow, and come to a gradual stop. One of my gloves had come off and gone hurtling down to the Vallée des Glaciers below. I picked myself up, fished a second glove out of my rucksack, and, feeling rather foolish, made the rest of the descent by putting one foot after the other. By the time I reached the Jaccoux, they had found shelter from the rain in a small crevasse by the side of a rock ridge, and as I climbed in to join them Jaccoux said, "What sort of game were you trying to play?" Michèle proposed that we have a little breakfast in the crevasse before going on, and by the time we had finished the rain had subsided considerably, although there was still a good deal of lightning on the ridges above us. We emerged from our crevasse and mounted a small rock pinnacle just in time to witness an absolutely breathtaking sight—right above us, a whole herd of wild, beautiful mountain chamois, terrified by the lightning, were leaping over the rocks, literally gliding in the air from boulder to boulder until they finally disappeared from view. We had now reached the last real obstacle before the frontier—a steep grass slope, made as slick as ice by the rain—and here again we helped each other along foot by foot. Jaccoux kicked steps up a snow wall in front of us, and by the time Michèle and I reached him he was stretched out on the turf, smoking his pipe, eating a piece of cheese, and calmly regarding the magnificent Italian valley that lay spread out before us.

The Col de la Seigne, on which we now stood, separates France from Italy. It is rich in the traditions of the Savoy. Until a hundred years ago, the Savoy—the whole of the Mont Blanc massif—was a single political unit; now it is divided among France, Italy, and Switzerland. In his delightful book *The Alps in Nature and History*, the Victorian climber W. A. B. Coolidge notes that even the summit of Mont Blanc (now placed, according to the latest Michelin map, in France) has been the subject of dispute: "As regards the actual summit of Mont Blanc, the French (and their official maps) draw the frontier line slightly to the S. (over the Mont Blanc de Courmayeur) of the culminating point. But the Italians (and their official maps) make the frontier line follow the watershed, and so pass over the actual top, and not to its S. Some of the older maps seem to be in favor of the French contention, as well as, apparently, the map annexed to the report of the Boundary Commission of 1861; but this last map is declared by the Italians to reproduce a mistake of the original Sardinian map, published in 1854 but later corrected. The text of the Report favours the Italian contention, stating that the boundary follows the watershed, and so passes over the summit of Mont Blanc." Needless to say, there are no customs officials on the summit of Mont Blanc, and Coolidge concludes: "It is amusing to think that the great Alpine summits have thus had divers political fates. This, however, was not due to any action on their part, but to the struggles of the human midgets at their feet, who were perhaps regarded by the cloud-capped mountains as intruders dividing up that to which they had no right save force. Till very recently, too, these midgets never dared to come within the range of the heavy artillery (such as avalanches) of the Alpine giants, which came into existence geologically before man, and may perhaps long survive his extinction."

The common language of the region a hundred years ago was French patois, and the language of the Italian Savoy is still largely French. Under Mussolini, the people of the Savoy were required to abandon French as an official language, but, as in the Italian Tyrol, where the people were required to abandon German, the policy was not very successful. The Savoyards, even with the political division, thought of themselves as a unified people, and among their most cherished rights was the right to transport goods over the mountain passes from one part of the Savoy to another. After the political division, this, of course, became smuggling, and the Col de la Seigne was one of the great way stations for smugglers. Indeed, Frison-Roche, in his book, recalls that in his youth he often stood lookout for smugglers passing in and out of France, and would receive a pack of cards or a box of matches as a reward. Now the col is on the regular route of the classic valley tour of Mont Blanc. By making our way to it over the glaciers rather than via the Vallée des Glaciers, we had replaced the two-day march around the end of the massif by a climb of only seven hours.

Our destination for the night was the Elisabetta, a beautiful alpine hut about two miles from the Col de la Seigne, run by the Italian Alpine Club. We were now on a broad footpath leading down the Val Veni, and soon we passed the Italian frontier station, a small stone outpost that was completely deserted and all but lost in the snow. When we got near the Elisabetta, we could see that it, too, was closed, and that we had no choice but to go on down the valley to the alpine village of Courmayeur, which is situated at the Italian end of the Mont Blanc tunnel. Between the Elisabetta and Courmayeur there is a jeep road, and we would have been delighted to hitch a ride, but much of the road was covered with melting snow and there was no traffic. A few miles from Courmayeur, we saw our first car—a small Fiat, crowded with people, coming toward us. It stopped almost at once, however, and they all got out and stood in a circle while a priest among them said a blessing over the mountains. He was standing on the shores of a small lake, which, I later learned, was created by a giant rock fall from Mont Blanc in the 1920's. Hoping that they could transport our heavy, rain-soaked packs into Courmayeur, we hurried to reach the car, but the group climbed back in and sped away without seeing us. In a moment, we came to a winding concrete road, and Claude and Michèle, arm in arm, set off down it at such a tremendous pace that I soon lost sight of them. When I caught up, they were stretched out on two wooden benches in front of a tiny Italian inn. It, too, was closed, but we cajoled a couple of bottles of sweet Italian beer from a girl who had been left in charge. A few minutes later, a rather magnificent-looking Alfa Romeo came along, and I managed to flag it down.

Until the opening of the tunnel, Courmayeur was an isolated village with a reputation as a summer retreat for the aristocracy. Frison-Roche points out that the Italian court used to go there for summers, and that young members of the Italian nobility were sent to the valley to learn climbing from the local guides. The occupants of the Alfa Romeo—a middle-aged man and an elderly woman—seemed to belong to this tradition, for they were extremely elegant-looking. But they had the air of people who had spent a lot of time in the mountains and, disheveled as we were, they were happy to crowd us into the back seat of their spotless machine, especially when they learned that Jaccoux was a Chamonix guide with whom they could discuss the mountains. There are guides in Courmayeur, but, as Jaccoux told me, it is a dwindling profession there. One of the reasons is that until fairly recently the Italian guide rates were so low, compared to the rates in Chamonix, that a guide could earn

a much better living, even in the summer, by teaching skiing. (There is year-round skiing on the glaciers above Courmayeur.)

The Alfa deposited us at the bus station in Courmayeur,
and we decided to spend a few hours wandering around the
village. It is, or was, a lovely, tranquil alpine resort in the
valley, full of charming hotels and restaurants and small
cafés. Above the town we could make out the rather ugly
road that leads into the tunnel, and we could see the dark
gash of the tunnel itself cut harshly into the granite wall. No
traffic was moving through, and the village appeared to me
to be living on the frontier between its past and a future that
would transform it completely. As it happened, we soon
had the first half of an experience that enabled us to measure the change during the summer. We knew of a nearby
restaurant that was famous among European alpinists for its
marvelous Italian-French cooking and for its simplicity—
the Restaurant of the Brenva, named after one of the glaciers
that come down from Mont Blanc into Italy. After our hard
day—we had been walking for nearly twelve hours—we felt
entitled to a good dinner and we went there. The food was
absolutely brilliant—platter after platter of hot and cold sau-
sages, ham, special cheeses in herb sauces, roast veal and
broiled chicken, red wine, mountains of wild strawberries,
and, finally, coffee mixed with *eau-de-vie* and sugar and
served out of a wooden bowl with three spouts, which we
passed around until it was empty. The restaurant was filled
with guides, tunnel workers, frontier guards, and alpinists,
and the price was half of what one would have paid in a
typical restaurant in Chamonix. The other part of our experience came at the end of the summer, when we visited the
restaurant again on the *fête des guides*, about a month after
the tunnel had been opened. The proprietor told us, with
great pride, that he had opened a second restaurant, with

the same cooking but with more stylish décor, for the new patrons that the tunnel was bringing through. We went to visit it. It was designed in excellent taste in the style of a country inn, with wooden beams that crossed under the roof and small dining rooms in every corner. The diners were so fashionably dressed that we felt a little odd in our mountain clothes. At one point, a parade of people who looked as though they had stepped out of a Fellini movie came down the stairs, and each of them took a turn swinging on the wooden ceiling beams. The sight of a beautiful Roman lady, dressed in the latest fashion, with her lovely, dark face illuminated by candlelight, swinging back and forth on a wooden beam said everything that could be said about what the opening of the Mont Blanc tunnel will mean to the massif.

After a warm bath and a splendid night's sleep in a modest hotel, we awoke to a brilliant sunlit morning. Jaccoux had promised us a relatively easy day. We were to take the bus as far as it went down the Italian sector of the Val Ferret toward Switzerland, and then we were to climb the headwall of the valley—the Col Ferret—dropping down into La Fouly, at the top of the Swiss Val Ferret. All began well. The bus careered along the valley, and we could look out at small country inns, tiny streams, and wooded fields spread before the vertical wall of the Italian side of the Grandes Jorasses, one of the highest mountains in the range. The bus reached the end of its run at a small inn, and we were able to persuade a family in a car to take our packs all the way to the head of the valley, while we followed on foot. As is so often the case in the mountains, the wall of the Col Ferret appeared, from head on, to be absolutely vertical. We could make out the beginning of an abandoned road that wound up the lower part of the face and then disappeared abruptly, as if its builders had suddenly thought better of their project. (In his book, Coolidge refers to the start of the construction of this road, which was to be a rival to the route over the historic St. Bernard Pass, a little to the southeast. I have not been able to discover why or when the project was abandoned.) We followed this road and then headed up the face, which was certainly steep enough, although hardly vertical. It was miserable terrain for climbing—loose turf that slid back after each step, giving one a disheartening sense of insecurity. Claude and Michèle were ahead, and when we were well up on the wall I noticed that they had stopped and that Michèle was sobbing uncontrollably; when I got closer, I could hear her saying to Claude that she was too frightened to go on. Claude was shouting at her to give him her hand, but she was too scared to do anything but cling to the earth. He finally had to wrench her hand away and all but drag her on. As they started up, he turned and said to me, in no uncertain terms, *"Je veux que tu ne panique pas!"* I indeed felt anxious, but I was able to get to the top with no real difficulty.

Later, I asked Michèle why she had panicked. I knew that she had been born in the mountains—in Mégève, in the Haute-Savoie—and that, as a member of the French national ski team, she had specialized in the most dangerous of all skiing events, the downhill run, or *la descente*. It is a race against the clock in which the skier goes straight down, or as nearly straight down as possible. (The downhill seems to run in Michèle's family. Her brother, Pierre Stamos, was on the French Olympic team and was one of the best *descendeurs* in the world.) When Michèle was skiing in competition, she would often attain speeds of over sixty miles an hour on terrain that was easily as steep as anything we had climbed that day. She told me that she had an absolute confidence in her technique on skis, and that on skis she would certainly have been able to go down the terrain that we had climbed up. But the sight of the long, vertiginous drop to the valley, combined with the unfamiliar, treacherous feeling of the terrain, had made her panic. I asked her if she ever got frightened on the downhill. She said that very often she was frightened, but that it gave her a special sense of exhilaration, which made her ski even better; this fear today, on the other hand, simply paralyzed her. The following winter she climbed up to this pass and skied back down with no difficulty at all.

At the top of the col, we sat down for a long rest and something to eat. We were now on the frontier between Italy and Switzerland. Behind us, to the west, the whole of the Italian valley stretched out, and to the south the countryside fell away into plains. In front of us was a gentle snow slope leading down to the town of La Fouly, which we could make out in the distance. We slid down the first snow slope, and Jaccoux spotted a system of snow névés—corridors of snow—which we were able to use, thus avoiding the rather tedious walk down on loose rocks. It was beautiful country, with huge cliffs and waterfalls and a rushing glacial stream that led into town. We took a path through some woods, and almost before we knew it we were inside a comfortable hotel run by a well-known Swiss guide named Xavier Kalt.

La Fouly is a town that still lives largely in the past. Kalt no longer takes climbers out himself, but he manages a guide bureau for climbers who come into the valley. Most of the people in La Fouly are herdsmen. As is typical of the small Swiss mountain towns in the Valais, they live in *mazots*—log cabins that can be taken apart, like Lincoln Logs, and moved. The Jaccoux had recently purchased a small plot of land near Chamonix and wanted to buy some *mazots* to move onto their land; every time Michèle passed an especially pretty one, she wanted to rush inside to see if it was for sale. Claude introduced us to Kalt, who turned out to be a portly middle-aged gentleman with an impressive beard. Apart from running his hotel, he was well known as a restaurateur, the specialty of his hotel being *raclettes,* a dish that is native to the canton of Valais—the area around the Rhone Valley. *Raclettes* are made from a yellow *demigras* Gruyère cheese, which is manufactured in the shape of a large wheel. To make them, the wheel is cut in half across a diameter, and the open edge is heated. The warm face is scraped off in a thin layer and deposited on small wooden plates. It requires a good deal of mechanical skill and physical strength on the part of the chef to keep turning out *raclettes* as fast as the guests can consume them. Traditionally, they are eaten with boiled potatoes, small pickles, and a white wine known as Fendant, and the chef stands by to dish up more *raclettes* as soon as anyone has finished his plate. I have seen people down as many as nineteen servings, but I myself find that nine or ten are more than enough. Jaccoux persuaded Kalt to make us *raclettes,* and after we had installed ourselves in a comfortable dormitorylike bedroom and had a bath, we came down to dinner.

In the dining room, we met Michel Darbellay—the guide of the boots. Although then quite young, Darbellay was already one of the most famous of the Swiss guides. He looks for all the world like the Hollywood notion of a guide—strikingly handsome, with an air of bravado—and he is known to mountain climbers all over the world as the first man to make the ascent of the North Wall of the Eiger alone. The North Wall of the Eiger is considered by many to be the most dangerous climb in Europe. It has been climbed many times—even in the winter now—but it still takes its toll of climbers each year. Three summers ago, Darbellay succeeded in doing it alone, and in a single day. Overnight, he became famous throughout Europe, and as one consequence he had a pair of mountain boots named after him. I was able to tell him that I had enjoyed wearing his boots but that they shipped water in deep snow. He and Jaccoux agreed that no climbing boots will keep out water indefinitely, and with that we settled down to consuming Kalt's *raclettes*.

Jaccoux had planned a very hard run for us the next day. However, Michèle's morale was low after her experience on the Col Ferret, and I was feeling a real sense of fatigue after three days of hiking and climbing following a long winter of relative inactivity. But nothing would put Jaccoux off, and the three of us settled in our bunks in the dormitory, prepared to get up at four the next morning, with Michèle and me jointly praying for rain; we had extracted an agreement from Jaccoux that if it was raining when we got up he would modify his plan. The next day, I was awakened early by Jaccoux, and after a silent and somewhat gloomy breakfast we strapped on our packs and went outside, Michèle and I being resigned to the worst. No sooner had we put our noses out the door than it began to rain. Michèle and I leaped around like two schoolchildren given a sudden reprieve, while Jaccoux peered sullenly at the dark clouds that were pouring over the high mountain ridges all around us. Jaccoux decided that we would wait for the first bus, travel down the valley to Orsières, and then take a second bus to the resort town of Champex, from which, weather permitting, we would climb up to another alpine refuge. From there we could make the trip back into France over the Glacier du Trient.

The trip by bus was through country as beautiful as any I have seen in Switzerland. This part of the Valais lacks the drama of the better-known Swiss alpine settings like Zermatt and Grindelwald, but it presents a wonderful panorama of deep valleys, richly wooded slopes covered with wildflowers, and always, in the distance, the great snow peaks. The town of Orsières is an attractive collection of cafés and *mazots*, while Champex, our last stop by bus, is a slick-looking resort set on the shore of a lake. By the time we got to Champex, the weather had improved to such an extent that we immediately took a swaying chair lift that carried us up over the woods to the base of a trail leading onto the Glacier du Trient. We expected to take about five hours to climb to the Cabine du Trient, a huge refuge run by the Swiss Alpine Club, and we broke the trip in half at a lower refuge that was filled with a large group of elderly Swiss alpinists up for a Sunday outing and in high spirits. We had a light lunch with them and then headed up the glacier to the upper cabin.

The trip to the upper refuge was along a gently sloping glacier. Normally, one ropes up on glaciers, but this one was so carefully traced out—a well-trodden path through the snow—that each of us went along at his own pace, which meant, inevitably, that the Jaccoux arrived at the cabin long before I did. "Cabin" here is an understatement. Like many of the modern refuges, this one was a huge stone structure capable of sleeping at least two hundred people in dormitories. It had an enormous dining room with a small alpine library, and like many such places, served simple but excellent meals. It dominated the glacier, and from the long balcony in front we could get a magnificent view of the peaks that marked the French frontier—peaks that I had climbed in and that Jaccoux knew like the back of his hand. Until we reached the Trient, we had had a sense of having the mountains almost to ourselves; it was so early in the season that we had met almost no one. However, the Glacier du Trient was full of people. The principal reason was that a unit of the Swiss Army—young men serving out a few weeks of compulsory duty in the summer—had come up to learn climbing techniques from a group of guides. I have been told by Swiss guides that this military training is one of the major reasons that guiding is a dying profession in Switzerland; so many potential climbers have had such excellent training in the army that they feel no need to climb with guides when they get out. While we were eating, the recruits, from all over Switzerland, began to troop in. Besides being boisterous, they committed a basic faux pas in climbing-refuge life, which is to leave the door of the refuge open. We were at about ten thousand feet, and each blast of cold air from the open door chilled one to the bone. Jaccoux spent several minutes ranting at the new arrivals, but finally he put on another sweater and did his best to ignore the chaos. In all, there were well over eighty soldiers, and since there was already a rather large group of people in the refuge, finding a bunk to sleep in became a problem. We were crowded in so tightly that I was constantly being jammed by someone's elbow or foot. About three in the morning, I gave up and went downstairs to take a walk outside. After some difficulty in unlocking the massive front door, I walked out on the terrace and was struck by the strange, heavy, hot atmosphere. The weather had changed again, and it was unnaturally warm. Lightning began to strike some of the peaks nearby, and when one bolt sizzled off a ridge not far from where I was standing, I beat a retreat inside to wait it out until morning.

With sunrise, the rain clouds lifted, and now the glacier was alive with light. Every few minutes, a gust of loose snow would be sent flying somewhere in the distance; clearly, a high wind was blowing. We had breakfast and, with a sense that we were now in our home territory, we roped up to cross the glacier. Jaccoux set his compass on the Col du Tour, by which we planned to cross into France, and the terrain looked so simple that, in defiance of fate, I said,

"*C'est de la tarte*"—a remark that I soon regretted. About midway on the glacier, we were hit by the wind. Jaccoux was leading, and suddenly I saw him tilt forward for no apparent reason, and then right himself. Next came Michèle's turn, and finally an icy blast hit me, bringing with it tiny needles of ice and snow that stung my face fiercely. At one point, Jaccoux stopped and yelled back at me, "*C'est de la tarte, eh, Jérémie?*" When we reached the Col du Tour, we found ourselves in the middle of a raging storm. I have never seen anything quite like it. All the colors were reduced to black and white—black granite and black clouds and white snow driven in great bursts by the wind, then rain with lightning flashes. The wind was incredibly strong, and it was all we could do to fight our way over the top of the col. Fortunately, the other side of the col, although steep rock and covered with loose snow and ice, was not terribly difficult, so that we were able to get down to the glacier below fairly quickly. Once we were off the ridge and again in France, the whole climate changed again. We were now immersed in a fog—a fog so thick that one could not see ten feet. Everything was absolutely white and totally silent. I had no sense of where I was or where we were going. Jaccoux, on the other hand, moved off with complete certainty. It was a virtuoso performance of blind navigation. Sometimes he would stop to look at the compass and sometimes at a pocket altimeter, although an altimeter is hard to use in bad weather, since the low atmospheric pressure simulates changes in altitude; even if one stands perfectly still, the altimeter will read different heights while the pressure is changing. Most of all, Jaccoux relied on his sense of direction and on the fact that he had been over this glacier hundreds of times. (He later told me that he had guided people in the fog over glaciers that he did not know by using a map, a compass, and an altimeter, and by measuring out distances and angles by moving one climbing-rope length at a time and counting how many rope lengths he had traveled in a given direction.) At one point, the fog lifted for a minute or so, and we saw that we had been following a perfectly straight path along the edge of a huge bed of ugly-looking, massive crevasses; Jaccoux knew that they were there, and he knew just how far away he had to stay from them. We were constantly losing altitude, and soon the snow turned into a heavy rain. Jaccoux began moving at almost a run, to get out of the storm. I was wearing sunglasses because of the strong glare from the glacier, which can oppress one even in the fog, and they had steamed up so badly that I could hardly see. I kept falling up to my knees into small, loose pockets of snow and being hauled out like a fish by Jaccoux. At one point, Michèle looked back and said of her husband, "Il a du zèle." Puffing and staggering, I found myself being dragged over a small pile of rocks, and then, out of the fog right below us, appeared the Refuge Albert Premier, above the Chamonix Valley. We ran inside the front door and out of the storm.

The rest of the trip back to Chamonix really was "de la tarte." We had lunch at the Albert Premier and, as a private joke, finished it off with tartes aux myrtilles, a specialty of the refuge. When we had finished lunch, it was still raining, but the wind had died down, and there were no signs of lightning. An easy trail led from the refuge to the top of a ski lift, and the ski lift took us down to the town of Le Tour, near the head of the Chamonix Valley. We stopped at a small café in Le Tour, and the proprietress, a friend of the Jaccoux, after hearing of our adventures, offered us a free coffee with cognac. In an ultimate manifestation of la tarte, we called a taxi from Chamonix and drove back to town in high style. A few hours later, we recovered the car from where it had been left in Les Contamines five days earlier.

Why make such a trip? In his book, written just before

construction began on the Mont Blanc tunnel, Frison-Roche wrote, "The Mont Blanc tunnel is going to be built—we have seen the first hole dug on the Italian side. We must hurry, then. We must hasten to speak once more of Mont Blanc, with its valleys which are so dissimilar in appearance and yet so similar at heart, before it is too late and before nothing is left of what made the homogeneity of the range, its old traditions. . . . To be frank, it is already too late! In the Chamonix Valley, tourism has triumphed and the cowbells are silent!" In a few years, with the tunnel, the cowbells will be silent in all seven of the valleys that surround the Mont Blanc massif, and our trip will be a reminder for us of the strength of nature and its weakness before the hand of man.

7

A Sense of Something Forbidding

When I first visited the Chamonix Valley of France, at the foot of Mont Blanc, in the fall of 1959, it was just under two centuries after the Swiss aristocrat Horace-Bénédict de Saussure came from Geneva to visit the valley, in 1760. While hiking to a subsidiary peak—the Brévent—de Saussure conceived the idea that Mont Blanc, which is 4,807 meters, or 15,771 feet, high and is the highest mountain in Western Europe, could be climbed, and he offered a large cash reward—about sixty dollars—to the first person to do so. (The reward, as I explained, was claimed by a Chamonix physician, Dr. Michel-Gabriel Paccard, and a chamois hunter, crystal collector, and alpine guide, Jacques Balmat, after they climbed the peak, on August 8, 1786.) With de

Saussure's dream, alpinism was created, and, along with it, the mountain aesthetic was invented. The English, as I noted earlier, transformed climbing from an expeditionary activity with an ostensibly scientific purpose (the pioneers like de Saussure felt, correctly, that they were exploring a new medium—high altitude—and took great pains to measure and describe everything they saw) to a sport practiced simply for the pleasure and satisfaction of it. By 1865, when Edward Whymper climbed the Matterhorn, almost all the major alpine peaks had been scaled by at least one route. And almost all had been scaled by Englishmen with Continental guides—mainly Swiss. Whymper and his party were accompanied by three guides—a Frenchman and two Swiss. Their accident, on July 14, 1865, while descending the Matterhorn, marked the end of the Golden Age of discovery of the Alps.

By an irony, surely unintended, future alpine historians may well come to regard July 19, 1965—a century after Whymper's climb—as the end of the Golden Age of the Alps themselves. On that date, the tunnel some seven miles long, drilled through Mont Blanc and connecting Chamonix to its Italian counterpart, Courmayeur, was opened to the public. The formal opening ceremony, which I attended, had occurred a few days earlier. General de Gaulle had been present, along with hundreds of tourists and Chamoniards. Some of the latter were apprehensive, partly because they thought the tunnel might jeopardize the alpine environment, and partly because many of them, like my friends the Morand brothers, who now own three major hotels in Chamonix, had borrowed large sums of money to expand their premises in anticipation of the new influx of tourists. (At that time, they owned only one, the Hôtel Mont Blanc; soon after the bonanza, they bought another, the Croix Blanche; and then afterward they built a third, the Beausite.) I recall the eldest of the three Morand brothers, a former professor of mathematics, who died of cancer in 1971, telling me in 1965 that if the family's gamble on the increased tourist trade did not pay off they would be in serious financial trouble. He need not have worried. In July of 1977 alone, 174,427 vehicles of all descriptions passed through the tunnel, and since the tunnel opened more than 10,300,000 vehicles, of which nearly 80 percent were private cars, have made the trip. The *Guide Michelin* of 1965 puts the permanent population of Chamonix that year at 7,966; it has since risen to 9,002. All the other people in the valley—hundreds of thousands in any given summer or winter season—are tourists. I doubt if there has been a single night since 1965 when any major hotel in Chamonix had a spare room during a vacation period, and for August, the peak summer month, many of the hotels are booked up a full year in advance. And at all seasons of the year the hotels and motor lodges accommodate numbers of people who are on their way somewhere else.

The Chamonix Valley that I wandered into in 1959, although I did not realize it at the time, bore at least some resemblance to the one that de Saussure, Ruskin, and Whymper had known. The names of the early alpine guides—Balmat, Charlet, Couttet, Dévouassoud, Payot, Ravanel, Tournier—were still the family names of the Chamonix guides, and were also the most common names on the local banks and stores. On the trail to the Brévent, a stone that Ruskin sat on while he sketched had been established as a sort of monument, although few people seemed to stop off to look at it, and fewer still to understand what it commemorated. The Brévent, to be sure, could be reached in a few minutes by a system of *téléphériques* instead of by a walk of a few hours. However, the major *téléphérique*, which reached the summit of the Aiguille du Midi, across the valley, was still a novelty, having been put into service only in 1954. There is now one other large *téléphérique*, which has opened up the Lognan-Grands Montets slope, five miles farther up the valley at Argentière, to thousands of skiers and hikers. The aiguilles—the granite needles of Chamonix—resembled, as they still do, the incredible spires of Gothic churches. By 1959, however, the alpine glaciers had shrunk since Ruskin's day to an almost pitiable state. As recently as seventy-five years ago, someone who wanted to walk on the Mer de Glace, a glacier that runs alongside some of the aiguilles, could, as I noted earlier, step out of the Montenvers, a nearby hotel, and be almost on the ice. At that time, too, ice blocks from the Mer de Glace would occasionally break off the glacier and come sliding down to the Rue du Dr. Paccard, the main street of Chamonix. Today, the glaciers are once again on the move—rising and advancing—and if they attain anything like their former size they will offer more of a threat to the dozens of new hotels that have sprung up all over the valley than any army of creditors. What did most to preserve the alpine character of Chamonix in 1959 was the fact that the two roads that led into the valley—one from Geneva, following the route that de Saussure took, and the other a steep, winding affair from the Swiss town of Martigny—led only into the valley. The Chamonix Valley was a cul-de-sac. Anyone who took these roads did so to see the mountains. The roads led nowhere else. Then came the tunnel.

With the opening of the tunnel, the Rue du Dr. Paccard—or at least that part of it which goes through the center of Chamonix—was converted into a one-way street. It is a narrow street, in many places just wide enough for two cars. One summer afternoon recently, as I was standing at the curb and waiting to cross, an incessant stream of automobiles, side by side, in pairs, waved on by uniformed policemen, swept down the street and off toward Geneva. They were bumper to bumper—all makes, with license plates from all over Europe. Because of automobile exhaust, a gray cloud of smog now hangs over parts of the valley. While I stood there, I recalled the rather acerbic observation of Ruskin, who as he grew older came to hate the tourists his own artwork had helped bring to Chamonix. In *Modern Painters*, he wrote, "I would that the enlightened population of Paris and London were content with doing nothing—that they were satisfied with expenditure upon their idle pleasures in their idle way. . . . The valley of Chamouni . . . is rapidly being turned into a kind of Cremorne Gardens." Ruskin was a thoroughgoing snob, and, to put it mildly, he failed to understand that the people coming to Chamonix in his day were there to study and appreciate "his" mountains. Most of the people inching down the Rue du Dr. Paccard last August were fleeing the mountains as fast as possible. For them, Chamonix had become just another way station on the map, and the mountains were, as they had been until the time of de Saussure's inspiration, simply a hindrance to travel.

If one sees a friend regularly over many years, one may not notice aging and other slow changes taking place in him until so much of the process has been completed as to make the change qualitative rather than quantitative. Since 1959, I have been paying visits of several weeks to various alpine regions of Europe at least once a year: often enough so that slow changes—a new hotel here, a new parking lot there— did not strike me until recently as introducing qualitative changes in the alpine communities. But recently, realizing that I had not really been paying attention, I decided to try to get a feeling for what has happened to the Alps. I was shocked. In Whymper's five great alpine seasons—from 1861 through 1865—he frequently traveled on foot from

Chamonix to what is now the Italian alpine village of Cervinia. Cervinia, which was known to Whymper by its
French name, Breuil, is at the base of the Italian side of the
Matterhorn, known in French as the Cervin and in Italian
as the Monte Cervini. Cervinia is about sixty miles from
Chamonix, and Whymper, who covered about thirty miles a
day in high mountain country, would make the trip in two
days. Such was the rarity of a foreigner in those parts that on
one occasion Whymper, having heard of the presence of
a fellow-countryman in a French alpine town he was passing through on his walk, had only to ask the locals "Where
is the Englishman?" to be led straight to his compatriot. I
would like to be present to hear the answer if someone
asked that question in a French alpine town today. Whymper used to walk over the glaciers from Chamonix southeast to Courmayeur and Aosta, from there due east to
Châtillon, and then due north into the Val Tournanche and
on up this valley to Cervinia—a somewhat roundabout
route dictated by the mountain terrain. Whymper was very
fond of the Val Tournanche. In his classic account of his
struggle with the Matterhorn—*Scrambles Amongst the
Alps*—he wrote:

> The Val Tournanche is one of the most charming valleys in
> the Italian Alps; it is a paradise to an artist, and if the space at
> my command were greater, I would willingly linger over its
> groves of chestnuts, its bright trickling rills and its roaring
> torrents, its upland unsuspected valleys and its noble cliffs.
> The path rises steeply from Châtillon, but it is well shaded,
> and the heat of the summer sun is tempered by cool air and
> spray which comes off the ice-cold streams. One sees from the
> path, at several places on the right bank of the valley, groups
> of arches which have been built high up against the faces of
> the cliffs. Guide-books repeat—on whose authority I know
> not—that they are the remains of a Roman aqueduct.

The present version of Whymper's trek takes about two hours. I made it not long ago in the company of Jaccoux and his second wife, Colette. Our notion was to leave Chamonix in the early morning, drive to Cervinia, take a series of ski lifts which leads up to the Col de Théodule, and climb the Breithorn, above Cervinia, which is widely—and rightly— regarded as the easiest four-thousand-meter mountain in the Alps. At 3:30 A.M. on what promised to be a fine hot day, we arrived at the French entrance to the Mont Blanc Tunnel. The tunnel is open twenty-four hours a day. Tickets are sold at both ends, but all the customs and immigration formalities occur at the Italian end. (Taking the tunnel is not cheap. The lowest-priced round-trip ticket available, for the smallest class of automobile, is thirty-six new French francs, or, at the present exchange rate, something over seven dollars. The tunnel, which cost seventy million dollars and took six and a half years to build, has already paid for itself and is now making money for both France and Italy, which divide the revenues.) At that hour of the morning, we were more or less alone, but if we had waited until eight or nine o'clock we would quite likely have been part of a line of several dozen cars, trucks, and buses waiting to get through. In August, the lines can extend for several miles on either side. The tunnel is reasonably well lit, is air-conditioned, and has a single lane of traffic moving in each direction. It takes about ten minutes to get to the other end. From the Italian end of the tunnel a sort of superhighway leads down to Courmayeur. When I first saw Courmayeur, it was a lovely antique alpine town with a long tradition of mountaineering. The highway now runs practically over Courmayeur. The town is still there, to be sure, but it has become a sort of appendage of the highway. It is full of gasoline stations, motels, hotels, and night clubs. Courmayeur is for most people a stopover on the way east to Venice or the Yugoslavian coast. Beyond Courmayeur, the road narrows and heads toward Aosta. We passed a turnoff to the Val di Rhême. This valley is one of the few places in the Alps where a government—in this case, the Italian government—has done something significant to preserve the alpine environment. The valley is a *parco nazionale*, or nature preserve, with no more in the way of development than one would find in one of our national parks. It is named for the mountain that dominates it—the Gran Paradiso (4,061 meters), a mountain often done on skis—and only a stone refuge constructed at its base indicates the hand of man. How long this state of affairs will last I do not know.

Aosta is now a dreary semimodern town, dominated by the sort of apartment houses so dear to city planners. After Aosta, one takes the superhighway—a toll road that leads to Milan and the south. The second exit from the toll road is Châtillon, where Whymper's steeply rising path to Breuil (Cervinia) began. Châtillon represents a more typical alpine village, torn between its ancient structure—narrow streets and old stone houses—and the exigencies of modern vehicular traffic. Whymper's steep path has become a steep, winding road overburdened with cars, and Châtillon is now a series of one-way streets designed to lead the motorist as quickly as possible out of the town and onto the highway. I was driving, and so did not have much chance to watch for Whymper's roaring torrents and upland unsuspected valleys. I was mainly watching for unsuspected cars, buses, and trucks carrying tourists and merchandise down from Cervinia on the narrow, twisting road. In fact, I was so absorbed in this activity that I would have missed the first view of the Matterhorn—it can be seen almost as soon as one starts up toward Cervinia—if Jaccoux had not called my attention to it.

When one makes the trip on the Swiss side, to Zermatt,

one does not see the mountain until just before one arrives at the village. The development of Zermatt is an interesting example of the kind of compromise that can be made to control the unbridled exploitation of an alpine valley in the face of an enormous tourist influx. Some years ago, the citizens of Zermatt voted to continue a ban on automobiles in their village. It is true that, with the exception of doctors' cars, emergency vehicles, and the like, automobiles are prohibited in the center of the village. But there is a huge parking lot a few hundred meters from the center, next to the cog-railway station. This lot, which is open to citizens of the village and to outsiders with permits, is nearly always filled with hundreds of cars; other motorists can park their cars six kilometers down the valley, at Tasch, which is connected to Visp, at the lower end of the valley, by a superhighway. Moreover, there is a bypass road around Zermatt, which is frequented by large trucks carrying men and materials to hydroelectric power projects being constructed and maintained in the lower glacial valleys above the village. Almost every available square foot of flatland around Zermatt has been or is being developed for hotel and apartment construction. The sound of the jackhammer is heard throughout the valley. Nevertheless, Zermatt has retained much of its original charm. The simple fact that the main street of Zermatt is a pedestrian walkway makes all the difference. It seems to me that where some restriction has been placed on automobiles people achieve a kind of harmony with the environment. The mystery and the beauty of the high mountains work wonders on the human spirit if they are given half a chance.

Cervinia itself presents a view that must quicken the pulse of any real estate developer. The town looks like one large hotel surrounded by parking lots and tourist shops. The reason for all this activity is skiing. Cervinia is one of the major winter ski resorts and *the* major summer ski station in Europe. One might say that no guide from Cervinia who was in his right mind would go mountain climbing, for there is a fortune to be made, at no risk to life and limb, teaching people to ski in summer, and the number of mountain guides has been steadily dwindling. When we arrived at the parking area near the lower ski lift, it was about 7:00 A.M. The place was almost literally crawling with skiers and their cars—hundreds of beautiful sun-tanned girls in the latest ski fashions, and whole families with their private ski instructors. I don't know how Jaccoux felt, but I felt like some sort of Martian, carrying a relatively heavy pack, with crampons, ice axe, and other climbing gear in it. Anyway, off we went, and two lifts later we found ourselves at the Breithorn Plateau, 3,500 meters up and 700 meters from the summit. The major hazard in climbing the Breithorn is not to get clobbered by a skier on the lower slopes. There were so many skiers that it was hard to see how they could avoid running into one another. The final slope of the Breithorn is quite steep—perhaps forty degrees—and by 10:30 we were on the summit, along with about thirty other climbers. The day was perfect, and we could look over to the Italian side of the Matterhorn and study the route that had defeated Whymper again and again, until he finally turned to the Swiss ridge. On the descent, Jaccoux, who for the fun of it had twice skied off the summit of the Breithorn the previous spring, kept muttering as we floundered along in now blazing heat and melting snow, "My kingdom for a pair of skis." We then took the two lifts back down, had lunch, and returned to Chamonix through the tunnel.

A few days later, Jaccoux and I made a similar climb above Courmayeur. This time, our nominal goal was the Tour Ronde (3,792 meters), which is a somewhat steeper version of the Breithorn, and which Mont Blanc overlooks. Again through the tunnel, and then to the lifts up to the Col du Géant, from which the climb begins. At the lift station here, the density of automobiles, climbers, and skiers was such that the lift operators had assigned each passenger a number to indicate which trip of the lift he was to take. When we got there, at 7:00 A.M. the second lift load—about forty passengers—had gone. By the time I was able to buy the lift tickets, the number was nine, and that meant about an hour's wait. By the time we got to the Col du Géant, it was 8:30. When we arrived at the base of the Tour Ronde, we were greeted by a bizarre spectacle. About a hundred alpinists—an enormous number for a small mountain—could be seen toiling up and down the snow face like so many ants on a snow-covered anthill. There was only a single path in the steep snow, so all the climbers were sort of in a line, roped together in twos and threes. It seemed as if there were a single human entity stretching from the base to the summit. (Not only the Tour Ronde but all the standard alpine routes are now overloaded. The highest refuge in the French Alps that provides restaurant service is the Goûter refuge, on the normal route up Mont Blanc. It is situated at 3,817 meters, and was designed to sleep seventy in relative comfort. About the time we were trying the Tour Ronde, a guide told me that he had spent the night at the Goûter and that 256 climbers were there. They were sleeping two and three to a straw mattress, and many were on the floor of the dining room.) Not wishing to become part of a human chain, I persuaded Jaccoux to tackle a neighboring Alp, on which, for some reason, there was only a party of three ahead of us.

While we were perched on the summit, it occurred to me that there must be some place in the area—apart from climbs that are impossibly difficult—so remote that one could find relative solitude. The previous year, I had ac-

The Dent du Géant from the South. (Courtesy of Bradford Washburn)

quired *Selected Climbs in the Mont Blanc Range,* a two-volume British treatise describing more than two hundred routes, all over the range. I am a little wary of British climbing manuals, because most of them have a tendency toward understatement. Following Whymper, I suppose, a number of British climbing writers use the word "scramble" to describe routes that for me are fairly taxing. After some study of the British manuals, however, I found an area that looked promising. This, too, was on the Italian side of the Mont Blanc range, and involved still another trip through the tunnel. So be it. The area I had in mind, above the relatively untrammeled Frébouze glacier, had no refuges with restaurant service but, rather, two bivouac huts—that is, small structures, usually quonset huts. The one I had in mind—the Gervasutti Hut, named after a celebrated Italian climber who lost his life climbing in the range—was constructed to hold twelve people. I took it as a favorable sign that none of the Chamonix guides I talked with—not even Jaccoux—had ever heard of the place, let alone visited it.

Jaccoux is always eager to explore the unknown, and so it was only a few days after I mentioned the Gervasutti Hut to him that we found ourselves heading through the tunnel again—this time in the afternoon, amid very heavy traffic— and up a small road off the main highway leading into the Italian Val Ferret which I had first visited in 1965, just before the opening of the tunnel, as part of our walking trip around the seven valleys that encircle the Mont Blanc massif. It was at that time a beautiful, fairly primitive valley, scarcely occupied, in which one seldom encountered a car. I expected some changes to have taken place, but nothing like what actually has happened. The lower sections of the valley are now built up with shoddy motels, night clubs, and restaurants. This was probably inevitable. It was the upper section—the more remote part of the valley—that really stunned me. The flat alpine prairies and fragile woodlands have been turned into tent cities—hundreds of tents attached to cars, with their occupants wandering up and down the road looking for distraction. Occasionally, one of these tent colonies was interspersed with dozens of automobile trailers. No one appeared to be dressed in any sort of hiking clothes; these were herds of city people in city clothes, who had left the cities to create a sort of tent colony in the mountains.

Our path to the bivouac started from one of these tent colonies, where, with some difficulty, I found a place to park. The disadvantage of visiting one of these bivouacs is that one must carry all the food and cooking gear up on one's back, along with the usual array of climbing equipment. My pack was so heavy that when I put it on I tilted backward. I gave it to Jaccoux to lift, hoping he would feel that a terrible injustice had been done in the distribution of weight and would relieve me of some of the hardware. After lifting it, he said *"C'est correct,"* and back it went on my shoulders. Jaccoux was carrying in his own pack, along with his personal gear, two ropes and a large assortment of metal hardware—rock and ice pitons, a hammer, and the rest—which he takes when he ventures into parts unknown; he was in no mood to carry anything more. After a half hour of walking, we reached the edge of the glacial moraine, and what had been a faint trail was replaced by a few isolated cairns. We met a group of young Italians coming down, but they told us they had not got very far up, and they had never heard of our bivouac, either. The British manual makes mention of "glacier confluents"—streams—and we had forded two small ones. Jaccoux had gone on ahead, and when I looked up I could see him sitting on a small ice hill and calmly smoking a cigarette. Not knowing how to interpret this curious sight—Jaccoux usually moves on at full speed—I made my way up to where he was sitting. He pointed, and there in front of us was what appeared to me to be a sort of Amazon among glacier confluents, swollen by snow melted in an exceptionally hot August. Above was a steep cliff leading to a sort of steep glacier. Somewhere on that glacier was the Gervasutti Hut. I knew we had had it. I recalled coming upon a similar torrent in Nepal, near the base of Mount Everest, where a team of Tibetans and Sherpas had helped us build an improvised stone bridge, on which we crossed. Where were the Tibetans in our present hour of need? I sat down on the ice and looked out over the Val Ferret. The sun was setting, and we could make out the tent colonies in the valley. Just across the valley, in a lovely meadow perhaps twenty minutes' walk from the road, were two isolated tents—people with enough originality to find a perfect campsite for themselves. To my right, below, I could make out the highway leading from the tunnel; it was lined with cars bumper to bumper. "Where are they all going?" I asked Jaccoux. "Nowhere," he answered, and we got up and walked back down to our own car. Another summer, we did make it up to another bivouac hut on the Italian side. It had bunks for nine people. Jaccoux and I were, as it turned out, the eighth and ninth. The hut was so small that we had to eat in turns. I had carted up the food—a couple of steaks and vegetable soup—which Jaccoux cooked on a butane stove. It was a marvelous place—conserved, no doubt, by the fact that one has to climb some twelve hundred meters to get there.

The Golden Age of the Alps was in fact a Golden Age for the very few. Whymper was conscious of this, although the *Scrambles*—which he published when he was thirty-one years old—has, when it comes to descriptions of the lives of alpine villagers of the nineteenth century, a certain hauteur. From time to time, one comes upon a passage that offers a real glimpse of what life in the mountains was like for the many. Toward the end of the book, there is a chapter about the ascent of the Grandes Jorasses—the very mountain under whose shadow Jaccoux and I had been standing. Whymper's chapter begins:

> The Valley of Aosta is famous for its Bouquetins, and infamous for its Crétins. The Bouquetin, Steinbock, or Ibex, was formerly widely distributed throughout the Alps. It is now confined almost entirely to a small district on the south of the Valley of Aosta, and fears have been repeatedly expressed in late years that it will speedily become extinct.
>
> The most sanguine person does not imagine that Crétinism will be eradicated for many generations. It is widely spread throughout the Alps; it is by no means peculiar to the Valley of Aosta; but nowhere does it thrust itself more frequently upon the attention of the traveller, and in no valley where

"every prospect pleases," is one so often and so painfully reminded that "only man is vile."

Whymper knew that what was missing in the valley of Aosta was iodine, which is leached from the soil by erosion. This lack of iodine caused goiter—an almost universal condition at that time in these valleys—and the children of parents with goiter tended to be cretins. (Friends of mine who grew up in the region remember being sent to the seashore "for their health" at least once a year when they were children; they were sent there for iodine.) This condition still prevails in the high Himalayan valleys. Now that the problem has been recognized, both goiter and its consequent cretinism are being rapidly eradicated.

Two other conditions common to the lives of the people in these mountain villages were grinding poverty and monotony. The Italian climber Guido Rey, who was born in 1861 and died in 1935, had a clear view of such matters. In his book *The Matterhorn*, he wrote:

> I can see in my mind's eye one of those romantic travellers of the first half of the century, come from afar to venture among the Alps, in the days when they were known only through the studies of a few men of science or the vision of certain poets. I can see him climbing for the first time up the lonely valley path, his mind filled with the dream of an idyllic peace, of a free and primitive life, awakened in him by the writings of Haller and Rousseau. . . . And already he dreams that the happiness of the pastoral life is about to be revealed to him. . . .
>
> But, when he enters the village street, he sees that things are not as the poet has portrayed them; a sense of something forbidding, almost akin to terror, is conveyed by the sight of the low, dark houses, huddled one against the other for purposes of mutual protection against the cold and of resistance

to the shock of the winds; the garments of the hill-folk are poor and ragged [some of my friends in the region remember their grandmothers' saying that they, or their mothers, had had only one dress, which was worn every day from marriage to burial]; their forbidding faces are never lit up by a smile; their life is a hard one, as is that of all things which live and grow in those high places, and man's fate up there is like that of the pines, which fill the fissures of the rocks with their deep-burrowing roots, suck up their nourishment from the barren soil, and grow in serried groups strong enough to stand the weight of the snows, and live till the hurricane uproots them or the avalanche sweeps them away; or else die slowly of old age when the sap of life is in them no more. No man notices that there is a pine the less in the forest, or a cross the more in the little cemetery.

. . . Perhaps the troubles and the worries that pertain to town life are not apparent in the mountains, but there is instead a sort of stupor, of dull, continuous suffering.

The summer is short: the rest of the year is winter, and the mountain dweller patiently awaits in his closed stable the sun's return; the time for harvest is short, and the work of gathering it in is heavy; the placid joys of labour do not seem to brighten men's lives in these high places, but hopeless resignation to fate shapes their course.

Today, one would have to go a long way in the Val Tournanche—the valley that Rey was writing about—or any other alpine valley to find a mountain dweller patiently awaiting in his closed stable the sun's return. That mountain dweller is, needless to say, teaching skiing or working in a bar in Cervinia or some such place for what his parents or grandparents might well have regarded as a fortune, and who can say which offers a more attractive prospect—the tent colonies and motels of the modern Val Ferret or the closed stable? Such is the peculiarity of human beings that it is this comparison, vividly apparent in the mountains, that confronts us in different guises wherever the automobile has been allowed to proliferate.

In the spring of 1975, something happened that, while it was minor in itself, may have set off a chain of political and emotional reactions leading to what happened in Chamonix during the very recent past. That spring, a group of eighty-seven young French restaurateurs attempted, as a publicity stunt, to organize a feast on the summit of Mont Blanc. The idea was that these young people, dressed in costumes like those of the early-nineteenth-century alpinists—who frequently climbed Mont Blanc with whole legions of guides and porters, carrying fantastic culinary provisions—would be flown to the summit in helicopters for an elaborate banquet. At best, the whole thing appeared rather silly. At worst, because there are often seventy-mile-an-hour winds on Mont Blanc, it might have ended in tragedy. In any case, almost the entire French climbing community reacted to the plan violently and negatively. Sabotage threats against the helicopters were reported, and in the end the whole project was abandoned, ostensibly because of bad weather. A great deal of heated debate in the newspapers developed over the project, much of it involving the mayor of Chamonix—Maurice Herzog, the noted French climber, who was originally from Lyon, and who led the 1950 French expedition to the summit of Annapurna and wrote a best-selling book about it. Herzog took the position that the alpine climbers—the French Alpine Club, the Chamonix guides—did not own Mont Blanc and so had no right to forbid the banquet. Be that as it may, because of the visibility of the project and the simplicity of the issue, the banquet proposal brought out all the frustrations that the people concerned with what had been happening to the Chamonix Valley had been feeling. Here was a small issue that people could get involved with, apparently to the extent of altering the outcome.

The banquet issue was trivial indeed compared with what was being contemplated for the valley itself. On its south side are the Chamonix aiguilles—the rock and snow needles that kindled Ruskin's imagination—and Mont Blanc. This side is heavily glaciated, and not well suited to ordinary hiking or to further hotel and skiing development. All the great climbing routes are on this side. The north side of the valley is dominated by the Aiguilles Rouges, a lesser set of rock needles, with little or no snow and ice. There are some small lakes at the base of the Aiguilles Rouges, and the whole area is ideal for hiking and low-altitude rock climbing. Some of it has now been set aside as a small park, and recently a good deal of effort has gone into preserving its environmental charm. The superhighway leading to the tunnel runs down the south side of the valley and connects with a small, badly outdated mountain road, which, in turn, joins a superhighway system leading to Geneva. Improvements to this stretch of road were completed in 1983. The alpine environment of the southern side of the Chamonix Valley near the highway is already destroyed. A number of large apartment and other buildings appropriate to a large metropolis have been built there and elsewhere in recent years, and many people find them extremely ugly. Most visitors to the valley drive down the superhighway, park their cars alongside it, get out and stare at the mountains for a while, and then attempt to drive into town, where—especially in the summer months—they create an impossible traffic bottleneck.

To deal with this traffic problem, the municipal government decided a few years ago to build a *rocade*, or bypass—another large highway, some fifty feet wide, that would avoid the center of Chamonix. The planners proposed that the center of Chamonix would become a pedestrian zone—something that the local merchants originally objected to but, according to recent polls, now favor. The *rocade*, how-ever, would run over the relatively untouched north side of Chamonix, the only part of the community that still looks something like an alpine village. On paper, the *rocade* looks quite neat, but its construction would destroy the last re-maining parklike areas in Chamonix, and trees a century old would have to be cut down. The *rocade* would pass just behind the wonderful old Roman Catholic church of Cha-monix, and then skirt an adjacent tranquil plaza where, in an old stone building, are housed the Chamonix Bureau des Guides, a weather bureau, and a municipal office that dis-penses climbing information. There was even a plan to run another highway through the Aiguilles Rouges, to bypass the valley altogether; this would destroy the whole area. If all this took place, Chamonix would be turned into one large highway with a pedestrian zone in the middle. And for what? Simply to make the area more accessible to automobiles—as if this were the basic objective in planning the development of an alpine resort community.

When I left Chamonix in September of 1976, the *rocade* looked like an absolute certainty. I was told that the bull-dozers would begin—and nearly complete—their work that fall. But in the spring of 1977 Jaccoux wrote to say that municipal elections held in March had completely changed the local government. Herzog was replaced by Christian Couttet, a native of the valley, and there were now four Chamonix guides on the twenty-one-person Municipal Council, along with a young Chamonix architect. The *rocade* project was being suspended. When I returned to Cha-monix, I was eager to find out why, and what it meant for the future.

The answer to these questions is not simple. But one theme did recur in my conversations with friends in Cha-monix: the people of the valley have had enough development. Apart from anything else, the development has been expensive for the community: the elaborate public buildings that were constructed were costly, and Chamonix now has one of the largest public debts of any community of its size in France. There is simply not enough money to build a *rocade*, even if anyone still wanted it. In the past, a *rocade* and similar projects meant "progress," and the general attitude was that such development was inevitable. But now there is a new spirit, indicating a change in the public conscience. I read, for example, a long discussion in a regional newspaper about the building of a new ski lift in the Aiguilles Rouges—a project that had been contemplated for a long time. The discussion began with the fact that the new lift would carry a thousand people an hour to the top—three thousand people by noon. The article went on to ask some questions: What are these three thousand people supposed to do? Where will they park their cars? Will there be enough room for them to ski? What additional facilities will be needed once they have arrived at the top of the lift? The report concluded that if such questions were not satisfactorily answered, the community would be better off if it did not build a new lift but merely made a few improvements in the old one. It was the first time I had seen such a discussion in the newspaper. And even if there had been one in years past, the conclusion then would no doubt have been in favor of the new lift.

None of this solves the problem of what to do with the cars and their occupants during the peak of the tourist season, but it does suggest new possibilities and new ideas. Perhaps giant parking lots can be constructed at the end of the valley, on the model of Zermatt. (In looking into this possibility, the Municipal Council made the remarkable discovery that under one of the newer Chamonix hotels a parking lot for nearly two hundred cars had been built and never used.) Central to all this discussion is the question raised on the occasion of the proposed banquet on Mont Blanc: Who does own these mountains? The answer lies in another question: Who does *not* own these mountains? The Alps were "discovered" just over two centuries ago, and the mountain aesthetic was invented. They have served the imagination of millions of men and women during all that time. It is clear to me that, whatever else can be said about who owns them, they do *not* belong to the present generation alone. We are holding them in trust, and, as trustees, do we have the right to destroy in a few decades an environment with such a history, and to destroy it in such a way that future generations can never turn to it to be enriched, ennobled, and solaced?

Selected Bibliography

EARLY HISTORY

Batailles pour le Mont Blanc by Henri Baud, printed in 1961 by Baud.
    This little pamphlet gives a fine graphic description of the early development of guided climbing on the Mont Blanc.

The First Ascent of Mont Blanc by T. Graham Brown and Sir Gavin de Beer, Oxford University Press, London, 1967.
    Brown and de Beer have written the definitive work, in English, on the history of Mont Blanc. It is a scholarly and delightful book that in many places reads like a detective story.

The Swiss and Their Mountains by Sir Arnold Lunn. © Copyright 1963, by George Allen and Unwin, Ltd., London. Published in the United States by Rand McNally and Company.
    Sir Arnold spent much of his life in the Alps and his book

reflects his love of both Alpine beauty and history. In addition to the Mont Blanc history, he also deals with some of the pre–de Saussure Alpine figures. These men were really not climbers, but they are fascinating to read about.

The Mountain Way by R. L. G. Irving. E. P. Dutton and Co., Inc., New York, 1938.

This book presents a collection of writing about mountains, all of it translated into English. There are sample passages from de Saussure and from most of the important climbers who followed him.

Mont-Blanc-Jardin Féerique by Gaston Rébuffat. Librairie Hachette, Paris, 1962.

Rébuffat was one of the greatest of the modern guides, and his lively and scholarly book reflects his own experience and his interest in the early history of climbing. The illustrations are breath-taking and give one a genuine feeling of how the sport has evolved and what attracts people to the mountains.

THE GOLDEN AGE

The Alps in Nature and History by W. A. B. Coolidge. E. P. Dutton and Co., Inc., New York, 1908.

A fusty, Victorian description of British climbing; delightful for its intended and unintended humor.

Scrambles Amongst the Alps by Edward Whymper. The Burrows Brothers Company, Cleveland, n.d.

Of this monumental mountaineering classic, one can only say, it is there, to be read and reread.

Edward Whymper by F. T. Smythe. Hodder and Stoughton, Ltd., London, 1940.

The most complete biography of Whymper that is available. Smythe's book gives a wonderful account of Whymper's later years which are not covered in *Scrambles Amongst the Alps*.

The Day the Rope Broke by Ronald W. Clark. Harcourt, Brace & World, New York, 1965.

Mr. Clark has taken advantage of the massive amount of information that has been put together about the first Matterhorn climb, and its aftermath, in the century that has elapsed since it occurred. He gives a lively and detailed description of what happened. It makes an excellent supplement to Whymper's book.

My Climbs in the Alps and Caucasus by A. F. Mummery. Basil Blackwell, Oxford, 1936.

This is as close to an autobiography of Mummery as is available. The book is written with wonderful good humor, but more of the man is concealed than revealed.

Vocation Alpine by Armand Charlet. Éditions Victor Attinger, Paris, 1949.

Charlet's book bridges the period between the middle of the last century and the present day, from the point of view of the Chamonix guides. Charlet's straightforward style and delightful sense of humor suit his subject matter perfectly.

Les Aiguilles de Chamonix by Henri Isselin. B. Arthaud, Paris, 1961.

A lively account of climbing in the Chamonix region from de Saussure to the present. From it one can get a clear idea of the role of Whymper and Mummery in the history of climbing.

Men and the Matterhorn by Gaston Rébuffat. Oxford University Press, New York, 1973.

A wonderful pictorial account of the history of the climbing of this great mountain.

Travels with a Donkey in the Cérvennes by Robert Louis Stevenson. Chatto & Windus, London, 1986.

A classic description of travel in the mountains in the south of France.

THE PRESENT DAY

Climbing Ice by Yvon Chouinard. Sierra Club Books, San Francisco, 1978.

The definitive text on the techniques of ice climbing.

Selected Bibliography

L'Aiguille du Midi, La Valée Blanche—High Points by Roger Frison-Roche.
   An interesting brief description of the construction of the largest *téléphérique* in Chamonix.

Premier de Cordée by Roger Frison-Roche. B. Arthaud. Grenoble, Paris, 1944.
   A novel by the first man not born in Chamonix to become a Chamonix guide. The novel reflects Frison-Roche's own education as a guide before the Second World War, when guides were trained informally.

One Man's Mountains by Tom Patey, Victor Gollancz. London, 1973.
   A true delight with many insights into modern British climbing.

On Snow and Rock by Gaston Rébuffat. Oxford University Press, New York, 1963.
   A climbing manual that discusses modern climbing techniques and is especially striking for its photographs of the Chamonix region.

The Mont Blanc Massif by Gaston Rébuffat. Oxford University Press, New York, 1973.
   A beautiful climbing guide to Chamonix. No other book gives quite the same feeling for the French Alps.

L'Amateur d'Abimes by Samivel. Librairie Stock, Paris, Delamain and Boutelleau, 1951.
   Samivel is the kind of mountain writer that could only be produced in France. This book, full of delicate humor, Gallic wit and real love for the mountains, describes climbing in Chamonix just before the last war.

Mont Blanc and the Seven Valleys by Roger Frison-Roche and P. Tairraz. Oxford University Press, New York, 1961.
   Frison-Roche describes, with the aid of photographs, what one sees if one makes the walking tour around the Mont Blanc, a tour that encompasses seven valleys and three countries.

The Borders of the Impossible by Lionel Terray. Doubleday, New York, 1964.

A wonderful autobiography of Terray, whom many people regarded as the greatest climber of the 1950's. Terray was the modern Chamonix guide *par excellence*. His life was devoted to the mountains and this book gives a superb and often breathtaking description of his adventures.

The Age of Mountaineering by James Ramsey Ullman. J. B. Lippincott Co., Philadelphia, 1964, 3rd edition.

Mr. Ullman is, of course, the dean of American mountain writers. His book gives a capsule history of climbing, including a relatively brief description of the origins of the sport in Chamonix. There is an extensive reading list at the end that will serve as an admirable introduction to the literature of Alpinism as practiced all over the world.